P9-DCN-014

WRITE THE PERFECT
BOOK PROPOSAL

WRITE THE PERFECT BOOK PROPOSAL

10 Proposals That Sold And Why

Jeff Herman
Deborah M. Adams

John Wiley & Sons, Inc.
New York • Chichester • Brisbane • Toronto • Singapore

In recognition of the importance of preserving what has been written, it is a policy of John Wiley & Sons, Inc., to have books of enduring value printed on acid-free paper, and we exert our best efforts to that end.

Copyright © 1993 by Jeff Herman and Deborah M. Adams
Published by John Wiley & Sons, Inc.

All rights reserved. Published simultaneously in Canada.

Reproduction or translation of any part of this work beyond that permitted by Section 107 or 108 of the 1976 United States Copyright Act without the permission of the copyright owner is unlawful. Requests for permission or further information should be addressed to the Permissions Department, John Wiley & Sons, Inc.

This publication is designed to provide accurate and authoritative information in regard to the subject matter covered. It is sold with the understanding that the publisher is not engaged in rendering legal, accounting, or other professional service. If legal advice or other expert assistance is required, the services of a competent professional person should be sought. *From a Declaration of Principles jointly adopted by a Committee of the American Bar Association and a Committee of Publishers.*

Library of Congress Cataloging-in-Publication Data:
Herman, Jeff, 1958-
      Write the perfect book proposal: 10 proposals that sold and why/Jeff
Herman and Deborah M. Adams.
            p.   cm.
      ISBN 0-471-57517-8
      1. Book proposals. I. Adams, Deborah M. II. Title
PN161.H47 1993
808'.02—dc20   92-29936

Printed in the United States of America
10 9 8 7 6 5 4 3 2

To all the aspiring writers
who need a little extra push
to make it over the top

ACKNOWLEDGMENTS

We are very grateful to our clients who generously allowed their exemplary proposals to be used in this book. In alphabetical order, they are:

Dianna Booher, Gene Busnar, Jim Castelli, Bruno Cortis, James P. Duffy, John Fanning, Barry J. Farber, Cindy Graves, Kathryn Lance, Stephen R. Maloney, Rosemary Maniscalco, Vincent L. Ricci, Jeff Slutsky, Marc Slutsky, Larry Stockman, Julie K. Walther, and Joyce Wycoff.

We have the highest regard for our editors, Steve Ross and Judith McCarthy. All writers should be so fortunate.

We received invaluable editorial, research, and technological assistance from Jamie Forbes. Any writer who needs a right hand should look him up. He's in New York.

Jeff Herman
Deborah Adams

My part in this book would not have been possible without the support of my friends and loved ones who have stuck by me through my own circuitous career path. I want to thank Robert L. Shook for showing me how to write my first book proposal and for encouraging me to push forward. I also want to thank Jeff Herman for being my second and most influential mentor by having the faith to throw me head first into the water, knowing all the while I would have to learn to swim. And I would like to thank my loving husband, Michael, and our three children, who all mean the world to me.

Deborah Adams

CONTENTS

INTRODUCTION

The Importance of the Nonfiction Book Proposal

The nonfiction book proposal is an important tool to help you arouse a publisher's interest and acquire a contract and royalty advance to write your book. At its best, the proposal can function as a sophisticated sales brochure. The more impressive it is, the greater your chances are of selling your book to a publisher, and the higher your advance is likely to be. That alone should be incentive enough for you to create the very best proposal you can.

Thousands of writers each year fail to find a publisher because they write mediocre proposals, even though many of them would have gone on to write successful books. The proposal process must be taken seriously; it's the price of admission to being a published author.

If you want to circumvent the proposal stage, you *can* write your entire manuscript before approaching any publishers. But such a time-consuming effort is speculative and doesn't guarantee your finding a publisher to buy your book. Furthermore, writing a full manuscript without a contract overlooks the chief advantage of being a nonfiction writer: if you write a proposal, you can sell your book and have a portion of the advance in your bank account before you've invested six months to a year of your time writing the manuscript.

The Contents of a Proposal

In a basic sense, a proposal tells a publisher what your book is about, why it should exist, and why you should be the one to write it. It may also explain why the book will be successful.

1

Through the years, a certain proposal protocol has evolved, and every proposal is expected to follow a roughly prescribed format. Fortunately it's a reasonable and sensible format that seems to work well for both writer and publisher. Of course, no proposal method is carved in stone. Many successful writers take creative detours with great results. But if you're new at this, it's probably best to start developing good habits by working within the conventional style.

In brief, these are the elements that a proposal is expected to contain:

1. Title page
2. Overview
3. Author background
4. Competition section
5. Marketing section
6. Promotions section
7. Chapter outline
8. Sample chapter(s)
9. Collateral attachments (optional, as an addendum to author background)

The sequence of items 3 through 6 is flexible, though if you have a particularily impressive background, you will want to highlight that by bringing it close to the front.

How This Book Works

When you look for a job you need a resumé to get job interviews. You can listen to the experts' rhetoric about the dos and don'ts of creating such a document, but nothing serves better than the books that contain a variety of *real* resumés. These samples clearly reveal each document's successes and failures—you don't have to reinvent the wheel.

This is the concept for this book. A book proposal is to publishing what the resumé is to the job search. By far the very best way for you to learn how to write a book proposal is to see proposals that have succeeded. It's a great advantage for you to see where these proposals were strongest and where they were weakest.

We have selected and critiqued 10 of the finest proposals on a variety of topics that we've had the privilege of working with. Each of the chosen 10 resulted in a publishing contract for the writer. Now you will not have to reinvent the wheel.

In walking through these proposals with us, you'll see a wide variety of formats, aesthetics, and styles of expression. But you'll also see that each of them clearly shows why it deserves to be a book. This exposure to a variety of successful styles will help you eventually to find your own.

Section One provides brief chapters that explain each section of the proposal and also gives advice on other issues you may encounter as a writer. Section Two contains the actual proposals. Some have been shortened to fit in the book. At the end of the book, you will find brief appendices of book proposal terms and suggested reading.

We welcome all comments about this book and look forward to hearing from you.

Jeff Herman
Deborah M. Adams
The Jeff Herman Literary Agency, Inc.
500 Greenwich Street
Suite 501C
New York, NY 10013

SECTION ONE

All Aspects of the Proposal— And Some Advice Thrown In

CHAPTER I

The Concept
Shaping Your Idea

A good idea is the foundation for any nonfiction book proposal. It's the intangible product you're trying to sell to a publisher. Good ideas are everywhere. But it takes a keen eye and know-how to shape an idea into a book proposal and ultimately a sale.

Finding Your Hook

What makes an idea good? Innovation and a focused target market give any idea an edge—or hook. Finding a hook is the process of taking a complicated idea and describing it in terms that resemble a "soundbite" teaser for . . . the next "Oprah Winfrey Show." Your hook is the focal point from which your book proposal can be formed. This hook must be intriguing enough to pull an editor's attention away from your competition.

As you scan the universe for book ideas, you have to find just the right focal point. But your book idea does not have to be entirely original. If you can write a unique or superior treatment of a particular subject, it doesn't matter if there are similar books on the market. If you're confident, innovative, and can meet the competition head on, you might have what it takes to convince a publisher.

The first thing to consider when choosing an idea for your nonfiction book proposal is whether or not the idea can be expanded into a book. Many ideas can sustain a CNN factoid, but not a 200 plus page book.

Some ideas can support only a magazine article. Magazines are good places to introduce concepts, but books require much greater depth.

Targeting Your Market vs. Market Saturation

Even if your idea can fill the pages of a book, the key consideration is whether or not anyone would buy it and read it. If you want commercial success, you must think commercially. The mating habits of obscure sea creatures may appeal to a certain segment of the population, but a book on the subject would not be a hot topic at most dinner parties.

If you want to write for the commercial market, you have to be aware of the possibility of market saturation on any given subject. When you're forming a book idea, you should first research the topic to see what's already out there. Go to a bookstore; go to a library and check *Books in Print*, a periodically updated publication available in book form and CD ROM that contains extensive listings of books by category.

If there are complementary books but yours can fill a unique and necessary gap, move forward. If you can't find anything that would separate you from the fold, move on to another subject. Don't be overly alarmed about books that are old and not currently being distributed. Many very good books simply have been ahead of their time. If a subject is important enough it can often be cleverly resurrected in an updated format.

If several books in your topic area appear suddenly in the bookstores— from different publishing houses—take this as a good indicator of market saturation. For example, after the first books on codependency appeared on the shelves, we received innumerable book proposals on different aspects of this recovery movement. While there are still territories yet uncharted, we found publishers were tired of the subject and reluctant to see anything more.

The Makings of a Good Idea

One way to spot a potentially marketable idea is to be aware of popular trends. But being tuned in to what is happening now is not enough—you have to be able to gauge where the public's interest may be when your book comes out. Nothing is more dated than a time-sensitive idea whose time has passed.

Keep in mind that the publishing industry operates at least six months to a year ahead of the bookshelves. Spotting trends and potential new markets requires an almost-visionary quality. You can get around the "I can't stand to hear another word on that topic" syndrome by being creative. If you can distinguish yourself through a new approach to the material, you can still write in a somewhat saturated topic area.

For instance, several years ago people involved with the "New Age" movement sensed that publishers were getting tired of their crystals and pyramids and started reframing their books in terms of "self-awareness," or "spirituality" rather than "cosmic consciousness."

Remember: Spot trends and then try to stay ahead of them. Spotting trends also requires a good understanding of popular interests. Do not rely on the electronic media to reflect trends in the types of books people want to read. For some reason, one does not offer an accurate guide to the other.

Popular magazines are more helpful in seeing developments in the reading public's interests. You may want to avoid the ones with two-headed dinosaur children on the cover, but magazines that reflect popular culture are a good resource for getting a sense of what people find interesting.

Trips to the library and bookstore will help you, but your greatest wealth of ideas will come from leading your life. Attend workshops and lectures that interest you. Pay attention to the questions people ask and the topics they focus on so you can get a handle on what kinds of books they might need.

Once you find your hook and begin to shape your idea, you need to look at it objectively. If it is a thesis that can be expanded and fleshed out to support an entire book, then review the following questions:

- Why would anyone want to read this book?
- Who is my target audience?
- What is my unique hook in 25 words or less?
- Can the hook support an entire book?
- Will I be telling my readers anything they don't already know?

For example, if you're like most of us, the straight details of your life would not sustain a book. But if you can tell a good story or spin a good yarn, you can certainly liven up your book with entertaining anecdotes.

Sharpening Your Focus

To shape an idea into a book proposal, you need to refine and polish it so it can be communicated in a logical fashion. Nonfiction writing is intended to convey information. Do not try to be literary. Concise and readable means no one has to refer to a dictionary after every paragraph. In nonfiction, there should not be several shades of meaning as you would find in classic literature.

Having a focused idea is imperative. An unfocused idea is one of the main reasons why a book proposal will be rejected. Aside from your hook, you'll need to state your expanded thesis in one concise paragraph.

If you can't convince someone of the book's merit in six lines or less, you need to be more focused. We've seen some exceptionally talented people waylay their careers with unfocused book ideas. Even the best lecturers and speakers in the world can't find a publisher for a bad book. If your idea would only lead to something self-serving or dull, give it up and start again.

You need to be both objective and flexible in the writing business. You need to be tenacious and persistent, but not stubborn. Do not try to force a bad idea into the system. If you become too emotionally attached to an idea, you may not see a better one when it comes along.

Sometimes a book idea has a gestation period of many years before it's ready to be born. Don't give up if some of your efforts never seem to go anywhere. Keep a file of good ideas that need more time to develop. With time, you might acquire the insights or ingredients to make them work. Let the book grow with you as you learn how to package and market yourself.

When you have an idea for a book, you should see where it takes you. Good ideas can have a life of their own when you give them a chance to thrive.

CHAPTER 2

The Title
Creating an Image

Coming up with a title for your work is no trivial matter. A smart title can greatly multiply a book's sales, while a poor title can have the opposite effect.

You might prefer to believe that what truly matters is what's between the pages—and you'd be absolutely right. But, when it comes to selling your work, your title has substantial power.

For a demonstration of how important a title is, stroll through your supermarket and pay special attention to the soap and cereal products. A close examination of ingredients and prices will reveal that most of the competing products are remarkably similar. When quality and price are essentially equal, it's title, packaging, and overall image that determine market share. Popular brand names such as Ivory, Tide, and Total were not selected arbitrarily. Companies spend quite a bit of time and money on idea bouncing, research, and testing to develop titles like these. They work because they trigger a positive image in the consumer's mind. The most successful titles, regardless of the product, bypass the intellect and go straight for the emotions.

That infamous automobile the Ford Edsel, which got its name through nepotism, not merit, was poorly rated by consumers and was short-lived in the marketplace. But even with good ratings, the car's title probably would have doomed it. The name "Edsel" simply doesn't appeal to the imagination.

Guidelines for Nonfiction Titles

Here are some basic guidelines to use when naming your book:

The title should be relevant to your primary thesis.　Don't hit the consumer with riddles or incomprehension. When scanning bookstore shelves, the consumer's eyes and mind are moving as quickly as any computer. Your book only has a few seconds to get its foot in the door. Develop a title that will make sense to virtually all English speakers and will state lucidly what the book is about.

There are important exceptions to this guideline, for which there are a variety of explanations, including luck. A prime example is the bestselling career book *What Color Is Your Parachute?* by Richard Bolles. (Initially, sky-divers may have thought this one was for them.) A book may succeed in spite of an incongruous title; but it's always smarter for your title to be an asset, not an obstacle. As a general rule, clarity is best.

The title should not contain more than five words.　A title with more than five words requires the consumer to start thinking instead of feeling. "What's wrong with that?" you may legitimately ask. Perhaps nothing. It may sometimes even become a big advantage.

But if the choice were ours, we'd go for the gut whenever possible, and leave the brains alone. Once the sale is made and the actual reading begins, the brain will have enough to do. But brains are not what usually spur people to buy things. Why would they? Brains don't even have nerve endings.

You need not feel overly constrained, however. Immediately following your title comes the *subtitle*. Here's your opportunity to elaborate intellectually upon your title. We've seen many successful subtitles go beyond 10 words. And that's fine—because, if the consumer makes it to your subtitle, that means your title probably worked.

The suggested five-word limit for the main title isn't a hard-and-fast rule, of course. Many excellent titles are much longer. Some titles, because of the subject, simply have to be longer.

Two successful titles that meet the word-count guideline are *Think and Grow Rich,* by Napoleon Hill, and *The Power of Positive Thinking,* by Norman Vincent Peale.

An example of an excellent title that seemingly breaks this rule is *How to Win Friends and Influence People,* by Dale Carnegie (seven words). However, those first four words pack an emotional wallop and win instant attention. In other words, going beyond five words can work if the first few words provide the emotional grabber.

The title should create a motivating visualization. Studies show that humans think in pictures—our minds translate everything we perceive into pictures. That's why it was never a contest between radio and television. The best communicators (and sometimes the most dangerous) are the ones who can make people *see* and *feel* what they are saying.

You want the consumer to scan your title and visualize your promised message in a favorable way. The book *Sales Power,* by José Silva and Ed Bernd, Jr., achieves this. Upon scanning that title, a salesperson would probably visualize gaining access to and closing big accounts. Such an image would be a motivating factor to buy the book.

For the same reasons, you have to be careful not to trigger negative or threatening images. For instance, it would have been a big mistake for Silva and Bernd to have titled their book *Stop Losing Sales.* Such a title would likely just evoke the image of the consumer's stomach and head hurting.

Titles for Biographies, Histories, and Exposés

Most of the titles we've used as examples so far are in the how-to/self-help realm. The rules are slightly different for titles in such areas as biography, current affairs, investigative works, and the like—though it doesn't hurt to apply the principles given above. You still want your title to create a dramatic and relevant visualization of the subject. However, impulse sales tend to be less important for books outside of the how-to/self-help categories. Sales for books in these categories are often driven through word of mouth, reviews, advertising, and publicity.

All the President's Men (about Richard Nixon and the Watergate cover-up), by Carl Bernstein and Bob Woodward, falls in this category. The authors' timing and credentials couldn't have been better. It happens to be a good title because of the Humpty Dumpty connection; but in this particular case, the book was not title dependent. It would have succeeded even with a poor title because the authors were widely known for uncovering the Watergate affair, the subject matter was timely, and the media gave almost obsessive attention to the scandal.

For a biography, a frequently used option is for the title to capture something personal and recognizable about the subject, and then to use the subtitle to identify the person by name. *The Last Lion: Winston Spencer Churchill* is a good example of this kind of title.

Titles for Noncommercial Books (textbooks and books for professionals)

The rules here are much different than for commercial titles. A slick title would probably be unhelpful—perhaps fatal. If you wrote a textbook for freshman physics majors, *Introductory Physics* would be an ideal title. For these books, staid, unprovocative, right-to-the-point titles are preferred. It would be unwise to name such a book *Einstein's Revenge*.

Final Caveat

Be aware that the title you create may not be the title your book ends up with. Publishers virtually always demand final discretion over titles. As the author, you have the right to try to persuade them, but the final decision is theirs. Publishers figure it's their job to know what works, and they legitimately assert that if they have to sell the book they should get to name it. But don't fret; they—and their savvy marketing staff—often come up with titles that sharpen a book's focus and boost its sales.

CHAPTER 3

The Overview
Writing Power Paragraphs

Almost every editor at every publishing house has a stack of book proposals or manuscripts waiting to be reviewed at any given time. If you start your proposal with a powerful statement, you can distinguish yourself from the pack.

The overview portion of your proposal is—or should be—that powerful statement. The overview is your first opportunity to grab an editor's attention and presell your idea. This first impression will strongly influence the potential for an ultimate sale.

The overview should convey these four major points:

1. What your book is about,
2. Why your book should be written,
3. How you plan to write it,
4. Why you are the best person for the job.

Leading with Your Best Shot

Writers are sometimes too close to their project to be objective about its presentation. They assume that an editor will read between the lines and see how great their book is going to be. Don't conserve your energy here in order to save the "important stuff" for the outline or the sample chapter. The overview can open—or close—the door for you.

In general, the overview should contain a synopsis of your proposed book as well as any persuasive material that supports your case. It's a sales tool much like a prospectus. View it as your opportunity to have five minutes of a publisher's undivided attention. If you had just five minutes face to face with a publisher, what would you say?

Your lead paragraph is important. There are many possibilities for a powerful lead paragraph that will catch an editor's attention. But powerful does not necessarily mean fancy, creative, or clever. In nonfiction, you are not trying to impress an editor with your mastery of five-syllable words or metaphoric didacticism. You are trying to communicate information.

If your book calls for it, you can use some of the same techniques you'd use in writing a magazine article:

- An anecdotal lead—one that tells a story leading into your book idea,
- A startling statistic that would support your thesis,
- A clear and concise statement of exactly what your book is about.

The last approach is usually the safest and most effective. If you haven't said what your book is about by the third paragraph, you're pushing your luck and trying the editor's patience.

Using Powerful Techniques of Structure and Style

Think of each paragraph in your overview as a soundbite of information. Each should be short and to the point, while conveying only one idea at a time.

Your first paragraph should be your strongest with each subsequent paragraph supporting your case.

The length of an overview can vary from two pages to ten or even more. It depends on the complexity of your subject. If your writing is tight, persuasive, and well thought out, detail will be an advantage at this stage of your presentation. If you tend to ramble and repeat pertinent points, then edit your material down to a shortened version.

Do not pontificate. Impress the editor with what you have to say and how well you say it, but do not include extraneous information intended only to impress. This usually conveys an image of amateurism and will dilute your effectiveness.

Take risks. Some overviews are so understated that they don't do their job of enticing the editor to read more. When you've found a strong hook for your book proposal, you should make every statement in your overview reflect the strength of your idea and the confidence you have in your ability to carry out the task.

After you write your first draft, put it aside for a while. Then look at it again and see if there's any way you can turn up the volume.

Some final points: Always choose active over passive voice in your proposal writing, and never say anything negative about yourself or your idea. You can't turn a bad idea into something it is not, but you can make sure a good idea gets noticed.

CHAPTER 4

The Marketing Section
Who Will Buy Your Book?

We know you want to write the book. But do we know who will buy it? In the marketing section, you will answer this question by justifying your proposed book's commercial existence.

For example, if you're proposing a sales book you'd want to present documented data about the number of Americans who earn all or part of their income through sales, and cite available figures pertaining to any expected growth in these numbers.

It's best to present this information in a visually accessible way, such as using bullets (■) to highlight each point. Remember, a book proposal is similar to a sophisticated sales brochure. The most effective way to communicate important information is to make it as easy as possible for the editor to absorb it without diminishing its substance. The more arduous it is to read something, the less useful it is as an efficient sales tool—even if the document contains important facts.

If you don't already know everything about your market, several sources can provide up-to-date and comprehensive data. Many public and university libraries have reams of government data on file, such as the latest U.S. census results. University research studies, private polling organizations, and industry trade associations are excellent sources for recent facts. You are expected to be an expert on your subject, so investing in extra research will not be a waste of time. The additional knowledge will likely be helpful when you begin writing the book.

Some subjects require a more extensive marketing section than others. For instance, business-oriented editors should already know about the market demographics for sales books. If you're proposing a sales book, your marketing section will be more like protocol than revelation to a knowledgeable editor (though you should always present it as if your editor knows nothing). But if you're proposing a book in a more obscure or arcane subject area, you'll be expected to go to greater pains to prove that a sufficient market base exists for your project.

It is rare, if ever, that the marketing section alone will carry or demolish the entire proposal. But there are definitely ways that it can either enhance or diminish the proposal's effectiveness.

Some potential enhancers:

- Presenting strong visuals that make it easy for an editor to glean and comprehend the facts.
- Liberally using genuine facts that are relevant to your subject and help support your expertise.
- Presenting relevant facts that even an expert editor may not know—and suggesting several potential secondary markets.
- Describing professional societies or trade associations that underscore the numbers and vibrancy of your targeted market(s).
- Showing an overall sensitivity to the fact that your book has to be "sold" to earn its existence—and showing an enthusiasm for helping to make that happen.

Some common diminishers:

- Claiming that your friends and relatives all love the idea. When pitching your work to editors (and agents), pretend that you're a hermit.
- Making improbable or irrelevant claims. Doing so will damage your credibility.
- Sweeping, unfocused generalities. Most editors know that there are more than 50 million adult women in America—but few if any know how many buy drugs to treat PMS.
- Failing to address the obvious competition. If you do this, you may appear to be a charlatan, sloppy, or both.
- Making stuff up. It's too easy to get caught—and it's not a nice thing to do anyway.

In the end, you want the editor to feel secure that your book won't end up overstaying its welcome in the publisher's warehouse.

CHAPTER 5

The Competition Section
What Else Is Out There?

Many excellent manuscripts are never published simply because there are too many other books like them already in print. "Great minds think alike"—whoever said it first, it's definitely true. If you have an idea, it's safe to assume that many others have had it, have it now, and will have it soon enough. Fortunately for you, only a fraction of those who think of it will attempt to turn it into a book.

In the competition section of a book proposal, you can acknowledge the books that are most similar to yours, and then show how yours will distinguish itself in the marketplace.

Making Sure You're Familiar with the Competition

There is a good chance your editor knows about the competition. If not, he or she soon will. Editors won't acquire a book before doing their own basic research about the competition. If the editor discovers that you've omitted some key titles, your expertise and credibility may become suspect.

Also, by knowing the competition, you'll be better able to navigate around it and create your own unique identity. Conversely, editors are quickly turned off by an approach that has been sung by too many others too many times and places before. No one will think you're a genius if you play copycat—even if it's inadvertent.

Take us as an example. We wanted to write a book about proposal writing (you're reading it). But we knew it wouldn't be wise to employ the same instructional formulas that others have already published. After some thought we stumbled upon an excellent twist that everyone else missed. The competing proposal books are rich in theory but poor in example—which is ironic, since we've always felt that the best way to learn is by example, not commentary. Using the wide array of sample resume books as our model, we developed and proposed a parallel concept for this book: lots of real and successful sample proposals supplemented by our critiques and essays.

In other words, while we entered a relatively crowded category—a situation that our research confirmed—we came up with a concept that has no competition because there is nothing else like it. We emphasized this strongly in the competition section of our own proposal.

As an aside, it surprises us that no one had ever done this book before. But there are many necessary products that didn't exist until someone finally made a prototype. The personal computer is a recent example. With that in mind, don't begin by thinking about what others have or haven't done. Instead think about what *you* would like to have to address the problem at hand. Eventually, you may come up with something innovative and useful.

If you're unfamiliar with and uncertain about the competing titles in your area, there are several ways you can fill that gap:

- Ask your local bookseller. Don't ask a clerk; ask the person who actually runs the store and orders the inventory.
- Ask your librarian.
- Check *Books in Print*, a periodically updated publication available in most libraries as well as many bookstores that has extensive listings according to category.

Turning the Competition Section to Your Advantage

If many successful competitive titles are in print, that means there's a healthy book-buying market for the subject. Frequently, once a lucrative market segment is discovered, publishers will step all over each other to throw books at it. This practice will often oversaturate the market's ability to reasonably absorb everything that's being published, and many titles will fail. Eventually things will settle down, and supply and demand will become more synchronized.

If you're proposing a sales book, for example, you'll want to mention a few successful titles that are among the most similar—and state the primary factors that distinguish you from them. Then emphasize that the impressive ongoing success of the sales category shows a vibrant demand for these books, and that it's prudent for publishers to continue to introduce new and innovative products for this market—which is what your book will do.

Don't overwhelm this section by stating everything that's in print. Many books in print are effectively dead as far as sales activity is concerned. It would be wasteful to discuss obscure or unsuccessful titles, since (a) they're really not competitive, and (b) if they're unsuccessful, you may end up condemning the marketability of your entire category. Instead, concentrate on two to six of the most successful and visible titles.

Dealing with a Lack of Competition

Be very careful. There are many subjects for which the book-buying market is exceptionally specialized (for example, horse breeding, managing mortuaries). If there is no competition, you don't want to leave the impression that there is no market. Instead, you want to make the editor think there is a sizeable *untapped* market out there that nobody has yet had the foresight to service. And by acquiring your book, the publisher will now have exclusive access to it. (Incidentally, there is a decent market for books on both horse breeding and mortuary science. But most of these titles are not sold in traditional bookstore outlets. If the kind of book you wish to write falls into a less commercial category like this, you'll have to seek out a specialty publisher.)

Remember that you want the competition section to reinforce what is special about your book, and create the image that your project will have its own place in the sun regardless of how crowded the category may seem to be.

CHAPTER 6

The Promotions Section

*What Can You Do to Help
Your Book Sell?*

The promotions section of a book proposal is the most difficult to assign a precise definition because it's often viewed as being irrelevant—in fact, some successful proposals skip this section completely with no ill effects. However, if you do it well, it can be an asset.

In theory, the promotions section is where you state ways to promote the book upon publication. In practice, publishers tend to do very little to promote the majority of the titles they publish. You are free to offer a rational wish list (including getting on "Oprah" and "Donahue"), but this is not going to catch a publisher's eye, unless, of course, you are already a regular guest or are a celebrity in your own right.

However, there are at least two ways to make this section go beyond pie-in-the-sky filler.

Specifying What You Can and Will Do

If you plan to use the book as a marketing vehicle to promote you, your company, and/or your cause, and you've got your own substantial budget to do it, then this section may be the most important part of the proposal.

It's not uncommon for businesspeople to buy themselves onto the bestseller list by hiring a public relations firm, buying ads, networking with powerful people, or buying a large number of copies of their book to either give away or resell at public appearances. If you are one of these people, then the promotions section should be a detailed and extensive plan that leaves nothing out. Of course you'll be expected to promise all this in writing as part of your contract; but you'll be able to leverage an above-average advance. While mainstream publishers shy away from obvious vanity deals, they're attracted like bees to honey to authors who have the wallets and egos to virtually guarantee their publisher a sizeable profit for editing, printing, and distributing the book.

Here are some other examples of efforts, less grandiose than the previous approach, that you can list in this section:

- If you're a public speaker, perhaps you can sell a significant number of autographed books at your events. State approximately how many events you do a year and what the average attendance is. If you've sold a large number of other books you've authored, you'll want to state how many.
- If the media frequently interview you for your expertise, you can probably get your book mentioned much of the time, perhaps even displayed on camera. List many of the important broadcast and print interviews you've had during the past year, and emphasize that these valuable contacts can be capitalized on once the book is published.
- If you're well connected and can get prominent people and celebrities to endorse and help promote your book, list them in this section.

Creating Innovative Ideas that You Can Help Implement

Any mortal can suggest a 10-city media tour, to which your editor will usually respond, "Uh huh," while thinking, "Fat chance, Charlie." Your challenge is to go beyond the usual and give the promotions section genuine teeth. Fortunately, you can pull this off even if you have limited resources.

To get your juices flowing, here's what other writers have done in their promotions sections (always be careful to distinguish your suggestions from binding commitments that you're prepared to have inserted into your contract).

■ Organize a contest relevant to the book.

■ Call up all the bookstores within a 100-mile radius of your home and persuade (beg?) them to stock your book. If you succeed, expand the radius another 100 miles.

■ Persuade large corporations to buy your books for their employees or to use as giveaways to potential clients.

■ Promise to get yourself booked on radio interviews (by telephone) across the country.

The possibilities of what you can do are endless. Showing determination here may impress publishers. They appreciate authors who'll work to sell copies—as opposed to those who only complain about the publisher's promotional deficiencies.

The promotions section can be like tonsils—a perfunctory part of the anatomy with no potency, which can sometimes be a detriment. But if you have real ideas and true substance to contribute, the section can become just the edge you need.

CHAPTER 7

The Author Background Section

Presenting Yourself in Your Best Light

In the author background section, you will state why you are qualified to write the proposed book. Without reservation or modesty, you should reveal everything that reflects affirmatively upon you as an expert, a writer, a promoter, and a human being.

How Impressive Is Your Profession?

As with other aspects of the proposal, the importance of this section depends upon your subject. For instance, if you're proposing a business book, it's important to note your professional accomplishments. Whereas, if you're proposing a lighthearted trivia-type book, the fact that you're breathing may be enough. In all cases, you should list any writing experience you have—even if it was just garage-sale reviews for your local *Pennysaver*.

For many nonfiction subjects, having relevant professional credentials is the most important consideration. Publishers usually prefer to have M.D.'s author medical/health books and Ph.D.'s author certain self-help psychology titles, for instance.

Even if it's not directly relevant, it's generally a good idea to list your career experience. That's one way to say a little bit about who you are as a person. Obviously, if you have an exceptional background or are a celebrity, you can use this to leverage a significantly higher advance.

If Your Background Is Undistinguished

As with the example of the trivia book, in this case what you can write is more important than where you've been. Simply say whatever there is to say about yourself without seeming defensive or embarrassed. However, if you're proposing a book about a subject that usually requires professional expertise, you'll be at a disadvantage. Your burden will be to prove that you have the requisite knowledge. Compensations include (a) a strong proposal and sample chapter(s), (b) strong promotability, or (c) getting someone with the relevant credentials to be your coauthor.

Additional Materials

In addition to the author background section, there are various self-promotional materials that you may attach to the front or back of the proposal. These include:

- A formal resume,
- Writing samples from magazines or newspapers,
- Publicity about yourself,
- Your corporate or self-promotional materials,
- Reviews or publicity about previous books.

CHAPTER 8

The Outline

Getting It Organized and Making It Persuade

Many nonfiction writers make the mistake of putting all of their energy into the prospectus portion of their book proposal package, and paying little attention to the chapter-by-chapter outline. The outline is as important as anything you will submit to a publisher—if not more so.

In fact, if you begin your process with a well-drafted outline, your entire book proposal is likely to be more focused and of higher quality than if you write the outline last. A chapter-by-chapter outline gives you the opportunity to iron out any bugs in your thesis and serves as a blueprint for the eventual writing of your book.

Tailoring the Table of Contents

When you write your chapter-by-chapter outline, begin with the table of contents. You need to focus some intense creative energy on mapping out your strategy. You can expect 10 to 12 separate chapters for a typical nonfiction book. This number will, of course, vary according to your topic, the level of complexity, and your book format.

If this is your first table of contents, you'll want to find a secluded spot away from distractions, and you'll need plenty of paper for rough drafts. You may want to prime your creativity pump by jotting down chapter topic possibilities before you try to put them into any particular order. Some people write chapter topics on 3" x 5" index cards so they can arrange and rearrange them until they find the most logical order.

Logic is the key to a good table of contents. The prospective editor must be able to visualize your book from a skeletal listing of chapter headings. One topic needs to progress logically to the next so the editor can see that your book will be well executed and complete.

When choosing chapter titles, keep in mind that clever is nice but clear is better. If your inner muse cannot stand anything less than a quotable phrase for your chapter title, subheadings can help keep your table of contents on track. Make sure to keep both chapter titles and subheadings simple and relatively short.

Writing Chapter Abstracts

After you complete your table of contents, you can move ahead to your outline. If you plan to write a sample chapter, you need not write an abstract of that particular chapter as well. To keep your outline in proper order, do indicate that the sample is included.

The chapter-by-chapter outline consists of *abstracts* or *synopses* of each chapter. The level of detail should vary according to the complexity of your subject, but it's always best to include more rather than less.

The typical length for each chapter abstract is two pages or less. If you make each paragraph count, there's no need to make it any longer. A book proposal is intended to be considerably shorter than a completed manuscript. If you include too much material, it may become counterproductive given the typical editor's limited time. Remember that this is only a rule of thumb. If your book is complex and requires more explanation, do not skimp simply to stay within these general standards.

A chapter abstract is an opportunity to show what you can do without having to do it all. It should be written in the best possible prose with an eye toward holding a reader's interest.

You can view abstracts as mini-chapters or magazine articles. The most effective contain some substance while explaining what the chapter will include.

It is much less effective to show only what you intend to do without being specific. If handled correctly, a chapter-by-chapter outline shows an editor that you can follow through with some solid writing.

Sample book proposal Number 9: *Heart and Soul* (page 143) is one of our favorite examples of what a chapter-by-chapter outline can be. The author has included the right mix of projected intentions, good writing, and solid content. The abstracts are interesting to read, well thought out, and substantial. They're not too long, but they don't skimp in any way.

If you put enough effort into your chapter-by-chapter outline, you could eliminate the need for a sample chapter. However, the reverse is not true: A sample chapter never offsets the need for an outline.

Remember that an acquisitions editor makes a decision to purchase your book or not based on what you present. It's best for both of you if there are no major surprises down the road. Stingy abstracts leave too many unanswered questions. You don't want to make promises you can't keep, and an editor doesn't want to take a chance on you only to find out you can't deliver.

Starting with what could be the beginning of the actual chapter is a good structural idea for an abstract. You might want to include anecdotes where appropriate and other samplings of your writing style to be more persuasive.

The tricky aspect of an abstract in a book proposal is to make it more than just a condensed piece of the chapter. It's an opportunity for you to continue selling your idea. This is your chance to shine. You have the editor's attention. You do not want to waste any opportunity to show what you can do.

Faith may be important to the quality of your life, but you shouldn't rely solely on faith to secure a book contract. Even the most worthy writers have to sweat. If you take the time to write a complete, organized, and focused outline, you will maximize your chances for a sale.

CHAPTER 9

The Sample Chapter
Proving You Can Do the Job

Understanding an editor's point of view on book acquisition can help you see why a sample chapter is so important. It's one more ingredient the editor can show to the head of the publishing house to confirm that purchasing your book is a sound business decision.

Would you want to spend someone else's money on you? Acquisitions editors are given the authority to spend someone else's money. Would you want to do that on someone's word alone?

A sample chapter is considered an addendum to a book proposal, but you should never view it as an afterthought. A good sample chapter gives you an important opportunity to further persuade an editor and to sell your idea. It proves that you can deliver and shows how your idea will translate into a book.

Show the best you can do. Writing a good sample chapter requires that you incorporate all of your best writing techniques. Your chapter must be well organized and well written. In fact, it should be the very best you can do. About 20 to 30 double-spaced pages is standard, but this will vary according to your subject.

Treat the sample chapter like a magazine article with a beginning, a middle, and an end. Make it your best work by taking your time and by polishing it as much as possible.

We can't stress enough how important it is to invest your time and energy into developing a good sample chapter. Your book proposal will help you hook an editor, but a good sample chapter will help you reel that editor in.

A good sample chapter will also increase your chances for a more sizeable advance. You are going to have to write a chapter eventually—so why not make it work for you?

CHAPTER 10

The Query Letter
Getting Your Foot in the Door

Once you've mastered the nonfiction book proposal, you need to learn the vital skill of preparing the perfect query letter. The query is a short letter of introduction to a publisher or agent enticing him or her to want to see your proposal.

If you don't have an agent, you're going to have to develop a strategy to get a good one. If you want to go directly to the publishing houses, you still need to know how to get your foot through the door and your proposal on the right person's desk. A well-crafted query letter can help you leap over this first major hurdle on your way to a sale.

If you decide to skip the query letter and boldly send an unsolicited (unrequested) book proposal to an agent or publishing house, you can use the same techniques for an effective cover letter to include with your package. Keep in mind that your objective is to convince the recipient that your proposal will be worth the time it will take to read it and that you are professional, credible, and worthy of serious consideration as an author.

The query is your first contact with the prospective buyer of your book. Be sure to avoid the mistakes that many new writers make and ensure it is not your last.

Up until now, you might have experienced a series of rejections in your effort to find either an agent or publisher. The problem may be in your approach, not your idea. Do not make the same mistake some writers have made of starting their query letters with "I'm tired of these people not wanting to see what I write . . ." or, "all these other agents/publishers have rejected me, but I know you will be different." If you were an agent or a publisher, would you want to take a chance on someone everyone else has rejected? Contrary to popular belief, agents and publishers have been known to give breaks to writers who might be considered long shots. Some of us do have hearts and can spot talent. But we are also human and not typically masochists. It's not good psychology to begin a query with antagonism or whining.

Think of your query as an advertisement. You want to make a sale and have limited space and time in which to do it. If you concentrate on a clear and to-the-point presentation of approximately one to two pages, you'll increase your chances of being taken seriously.

The goal of your query letter is to pique the interest of an editor who has very little time and probably very little patience. You want to entice him or her to ask for more.

The Query Package

You can put together what is called a query package. It should include your query letter, a short resume, and media clippings or other favorable documents. Do not get carried away. Photographs of your children and pets or certificates of merit from local writing contests should not be included. Don't waste space in your query describing all of your supporting materials. You can state at the bottom of your letter that there are enclosures or refer to them in a general sense in your introductory material. For example: "Enclosed are some supporting materials."

Include a self-addressed stamped envelope (SASE) with enough postage to return your entire package. This will be particularly appreciated by smaller publishing houses and independent agents.

Query/cover letters follow a simple format that can be reworked according to your individual preferences:

1. Lead,
2. Supporting material/persuasion,
3. Biography,
4. Conclusion/pitch.

Your Lead Is Your Hook

The lead paragraph in your query letter can either catch an editor's attention or turn her or him off completely. Writers sometimes mistakenly think that they have to do something dramatic to get someone's attention in a short space. If you're clever enough (do not take this as a challenge), a creative lead can be impressive, but it's safer to opt for clearly conveying thoroughly developed ideas. Get right to the point. The recipient of your letter shouldn't get the impression that you slaved over every word. That person really just wants to know why you're writing and what you have to offer.

Do not play it so safe, though, that you appear boring, stuffy, and factual. Determine what is most important about the book you're trying to sell and put this hook front and center.

The journalistic inverted pyramid is a good technique for a query letter. You begin with your strongest material and back it up with details in the subsequent paragraphs. It generally works better than beginning your letter slowly and picking up momentum as you go along.

Some possibilities for your lead paragraph are: using an anecdote; making a statement of fact(s); or using a question, a comparison, or a provocative relevant statistic.

Some writers tend to make glowing statements about the book's potential in the first paragraph without ever directly stating what the book is about. Remember that the most important bit of information you're trying to convey in your lead is the thesis of your proposal. Your letter may never be read beyond the lead if you do not have a solid hook.

Avoid bad jokes, clichés, unsubstantiated claims, and dictionary definitions in your lead. They're not effective and will make you appear amateurish.

Never be condescending; editors have egos, too, and have the power to influence your future.

Supporting Material: Be Persuasive

After your lead, you'll want to include supporting material to substantiate your main idea. This could include some preliminary research or strong, convincing statements to back up your thesis.

This is also the portion of your query where you convince an agent or editor why your book should exist. Your goal is to sell your topic and your credentials while showing that you can back up your claims.

It's certainly acceptable to include a separate table of contents with your enclosures, but don't include this in the body of your letter.

If your query is directed to a publishing house, you could include a few lines demonstrating what the publisher will gain from the project. If you have brilliant and novel ideas for marketing that are realistic, include them.

It can be highly effective to state specific and unique avenues you might have for selling the book. Although the query contains much less detail than your book proposal, don't assume that editors will get the big picture later. If you don't entice them with your query, they'll never see the full proposal.

When rereading your letter, make sure you've shown that you understand your own idea thoroughly. Don't expect an editor to take the time to help you flesh out your thoughts. Exude confidence without being cocky, and make sure everything is grammatically correct.

Your Biography Is No Place for Modesty

The biographical information in your letter can be interspersed with, or placed separately after, your supporting material. Remember to toot your own horn in a carefully calculated persuasive fashion. Include only relevant credentials that support the sale of your book. Don't waste space in your letter on too many extraneous details.

If, in order to be credible, your nonfiction book idea requires expertise, focus your biography on those qualifications that make you or a member of your writing team the best person to write this particular book.

You are not trying to impress anyone with how great a person you are. You are trying to show them you are qualified to do a particular job. The third-grade writing competition might have made your mother proud, but it has no relevance here.

Don't overlook nonacademic credentials that might correspond to your book topic. Often those experiences are more valuable than academic accomplishments. Any media or public-speaking experience should certainly be highlighted.

There's no room for humility or modesty in the query letter. You need to find some way to make yourself compelling as an author in the same way ad agencies find ways to create excitement about toothpaste and other products.

Here's the Pitch

In the closing of your letter, reel them in. This means asking directly for the result you want: representation or a sale. Use strong statements like "I look forward to your speedy response." Do not hedge with phrases such as "I hope" or "I think you will like my book, but I'm not sure." This may be your only opportunity to go for the kill, and you have nothing to lose. Be sure to thank the editor or agent for his or her attention.

Finishing Touches

Edit . . . edit . . . edit.

Make sure your letter is aesthetically appealing. Use good letterhead paper and only black ink in your typewriter ribbon or printer. Your letter should represent you in the best possible way.

CHAPTER 11

An Agent's Advice
Career Development and Financial Success

The nonfiction book proposal is just one important tool for your writing career. Learning to use it well will give you the professional edge that will set you above the competition. But there's a lot more to building a successful writing career than mastering the proposal craft. You must take charge of your career, and learn how to get the largest possible advances to support yourself.

Charting Your Writing Career

Writing careers are created. You can take the lottery approach, as one editor described it, which is to buy a ticket and hope for fame, glory, and cash through sheer luck of the draw. Or you can be in charge of your career, mapping out your course with precision and forethought.

If you're writing to enhance a primary professional career, you'll develop a strategy much different than if you're writing because you simply love to write. Psychologists, medical doctors, lawyers, and other professionals see writing a book as a means to build name recognition and a reputation as an expert in a particular area.

If you fall within this category, you'll enhance your chances of being published if you work on building your reputation before writing a book.

You need to speak or write at every opportunity as well as to try carving out a particular niche that only you can fill. Specialization is the key.

For example, you may be the greatest psychologist in the world, but if you don't have an area of expertise or hook that can be summed up in a 30-second spot on "Oprah" as the "syndrome of the week," you aren't going to be able to publish a book in the commercial market.

If you want to write for the sake of writing, you need to recognize that wanting and doing are two entirely different matters. A career in writing requires self-motivation and very thick skin. Even if you think you have what it takes, our first bit of advice to you is: Don't immediately sell your belongings and move into a loft, and don't give up your day job unless you have a sizeable trust fund. You want to be in control of your career. It's difficult to be enthusiastic and creative when you're scraping the bottom of your change drawer to buy dry spaghetti and a jar of Ragú.

It's easy to be unrealistic about the monetary potential of a writing career when you're motivated and bursting with enthusiasm. This book can help you skip some of the dues necessary to make your career solely as a writer. But you have to expect that it could take some time for you to develop a system that will keep you in the cash flow.

A writing career can be monetarily rewarding, and you should always believe in your potential. You merely want to have a back-up system to allow for the unexpected at the early stages of your career.

Even if you have a job you don't particularly love, you can use your free time to write as much as possible. Freelance writing and editing for magazines or public relations firms is a great way to build your credentials. Publishers want to feel confident that you can deliver what you promise. A solid clipping file shows a proven track record. Experience is also an advantage of an active freelancing career. The more you write, the better you become.

Once you choose to write full time without any other source of income, our second bit of advice is: Learn to budget. This means time as well as money—but mostly money. If you want to write books for a living, you should learn to anticipate two months of circulation time to sell a book proposal to a publisher, if you are so lucky. Then expect it to take six weeks after that to get the contract, and six more weeks to get the first half of the advance.

The second half of your advance generally is paid when the publisher approves the manuscript for publication. This will depend on your deadline; some are nine months to a year. Royalties? Books are always purchased at least a year before they're expected to reach the shelves. If your book earns back its advance, you still will not see royalties for quite some time.

Sowing Your Seeds Wisely and Widely

Smart writers stagger assignments and are always planting seeds for new projects. The more seeds you plant, the less time you'll spend contemplating marrying for money or running home to Mom and Dad.

If you choose to be a writer, whether or not you're actively in the business, *think* of yourself as a writer. View everything you do as an opportunity for new material. Look at the world with a critical eye, and always think in terms of trends and filling an information need for the mass audience.

Attending writers' conferences and workshops and joining writers' groups can be great ways to get your career off the ground. But a word of caution: Watch out for aspiring writers who like to build their careers by knocking out any perceived competition. They do it by psyching you out so you won't have the confidence to write a grocery list. If someone who is not a personal friend shows too much interest in what you're doing—be suspicious. You do not want anyone knowing your vulnerabilities. One "Oh, haven't you sold that book yet?" and you are deflated.

And ignore how many great publishers are interested in someone else's work if this kind of comparison makes you feel inadequate. It's most likely a crock of you-know-what anyway.

True writers' friends have enough experience to be secure within themselves. They'll give tips freely and will revel in your achievements. They are the writers who have seen a measure of their own success and who have a bit of seasoning. Don't kid yourself: No matter how successful writers become, it's difficult to resist some starry-eyed neophyte looking at them like they're demigods. Ask for help and follow up on any good advice or potential contacts.

Packaging Your Product—You

The best way to take charge of your career is to view yourself as a business, with *you* as the main product. Think about how you can best package yourself. Treat yourself with respect and take yourself seriously even if no one else does.

Above all else, have endurance. Some people get a sale the first time around and can learn as they go. Others have to learn the business by surviving rejection after rejection. Rejection is just a part of research and development. You need to refine your product until it's just right for the market.

Use your brain. Luck may be a part of everything in life, but a strategic approach raises the odds that you will succeed in the career you have chosen. You may lack experience, but anyone can improve with practice and objective self-evaluation.

Do not sabotage yourself with impatience. The worst thing you can do is to make a nuisance of yourself. If you call an agent or editor one day after they would have received your proposal, you're going to be seen as a potential "pain in the __ __ __." The next time you call, you might find that they're in a permanent meeting.

Your career may mean everything to you, but the writing business progresses in its own time. Keep yourself busy so you're not sitting by the telephone or mailbox. Who knows? Maybe someday the publishers will be waiting for you.

Landing a Bigger Book Advance

There are several strategies that can help to increase the worth of your book in your prospective publisher's eyes. The best advice we can give to obtain a bigger book advance is to find a good agent. However, finding an agent may be as tricky as finding a publisher. If you are unable to get past this proverbial Catch-22 at this stage of your career, there are several things you can do to improve your bargaining position with any publisher.

First you need to understand what is meant by an advance and what purpose it serves for both writer and publisher.

What Is an Advance?

The advance is the upfront money the publisher pays the writer in exchange for the right to publish his or her book upon its completion.

The publisher is eventually repaid the advance money through the writer's future royalty and subsidiary rights income, if the book earns enough to make this possible. The writer is not required to return any money if the book does not recoup the advance, so the advance is essentially the money a publisher is willing to risk for the chance to publish your book.

If, for example, you receive a $10,000 advance for your book, you will not receive any more money until your share of the book's income exceeds $10,000.

What Does the Size of the Advance Mean?

The size of the advance is usually determined by what the publisher predicts the writer is likely to earn within the book's first year in print.

The advance is also a rough indication of how much attention and support the book will receive from the publisher. Naturally, the publisher will be much more concerned about the book for which it paid $100,000 than the one for which it paid $5,000.

There are no set rules in the advance game. Some publishers are stingy across the board, and small presses and university houses often don't have a lot of capital to speculate with. Many books never come close to earning back their advances, while other books perform well beyond anyone's expectations and earn back the advance several times.

That's why determining the advance is one of the most arbitrary aspects of the acquisition process.

The Writer's Road to Bigger Advances

Publishers are willing to pay a price that equals a perceived value. It's the writer's job to package herself and her material effectively, and to project as much potential value for the book as possible. There are several tangible and subliminal ways to accomplish this. The most obvious is to have good materials and credentials. A less obvious way is to radiate a persona of confidence, professionalism, and an overall winning image.

Here are methods you can employ to enhance the possibility of getting a higher advance:

Understand the contract—and negotiate. You don't have to accept the publisher's first offer. This may be the editor and publisher you want to work with, and that's fine. But you can still negotiate with them for better terms.

The first offer is rarely the final offer. Publishers, like all buyers in all businesses, will tend to offer what they think they can get away with. You have to show them what they *can't* get away with.

There are no set negotiating rules, but a little knowledge could get you a bigger advance. Before you even begin the submission process, we suggest you buy and read *How to Understand and Negotiate a Book Contract*, by Richard Balkin (Writer's Digest Books) and *The Writer's Legal Companion*, by Brad Bunnin and Peter Beren (Addison-Wesley). Both books will walk you through the typical book contract. No two publishers have identical contracts, but they do all contain similar provisions.

It's important for writers to recognize that every contract has "soft" and "hard" areas, meaning contractual aspects that the publisher expects give-and-take on, and aspects that can rarely be hedged by anyone.

Let's say an editor calls to say the publishing house wants to acquire your work and is prepared to pay you a $5,000 advance. Follow these steps:

First, ask questions:

- Find out in what format the publisher intends to publish the book (hardback, mass market, or quality paperback). Each format tends to have a different royalty schedule, with hardcover earning the highest percentages and trade paperbacks earning the lowest. However, paperbacks often achieve greater sales volumes, thereby offsetting and perhaps surpassing the per-unit royalty difference.

- Find out whether the publisher pays royalties against list price or net receipts. This will make a big difference in your bottom line. If the royalty is paid against list (the cover price), you'll know exactly what you're getting per sold copy. However, when you're paid against the publisher's net, your royalty is assessed against what the publisher receives per copy, which due to sales discounts can fluctuate between 40 and 50 percent of the list price. Obviously, your income will be higher (on a per-book basis) and more predictable when paid against list. To offset this, some publishers that pay on net will pay higher royalty percentages than the publishers that pay on list.

- Find out how large a first printing the publisher plans. (This may not be determined until much later.) The first printing will reveal the number of copies the publisher believes it can realistically sell within the first few months of publication.

- Find out what the publisher's "standard" royalty schedules are. Although each publisher has its own "usual schedule," the good houses tend to approximate each other. The typical hardcover schedule is 10 percent on the first 5,000 copies sold, $12\frac{1}{2}$ percent on the second 5,000 copies, and 15 percent thereafter. Trade paperbacks tend to range anywhere from 6 to $8\frac{1}{2}$ percent, and mass market from 8 to 10 percent. (These figures assume that royalties are paid against list price.) Depending on the situation, these percentages are open to discussion during the contract negotiations.

- Find out what subsidiary rights the publisher wants to keep and what percent of such sales would be paid to you. The most common subsidiary rights are translation, world English, audio/video, software/electronic/CD-ROM, dramatization, and first and second serial rights. Retain these rights only if you intend to peddle them. Otherwise, if your publisher has an active subsidiary rights department, assign them to your publisher and negotiate favorable percentages of the income. Depending upon the right in question and the publisher's customary schedules, you can secure anywhere from 50 percent to 90 percent of the income pertaining to each right.

All these factors will influence your royalties down the road and should be taken into account when determining a fair advance. However, the publisher may not yet have definitive answers to all of these questions.

Second, say as little as possible: If you commit yourself too soon, you run the risk of binding yourself to an unfair situation, one the publisher would have been willing to negotiate. Buy yourself a few days to get educated and then come back once you know what you're dealing with.

Third, find out everything you can: Seek advice from experienced friends and colleagues. Try to talk to other people who write for the same publisher. See if their terms match yours.

Let's say you've discovered that the publisher tends to pay considerably more than the $5,000 advance offered you—perhaps $15,000 for books that are similar to yours. So, once you're confident and ready to play, call the publisher back and request $20,000 or more and the game begins. Always be courteous, professional, and flexible. But remember, the publisher may not want to pay more than $5,000 for your book, period.

Get noteworthy people to promise endorsements or a foreword. How often do you pick up a book in a store and feel impressed by the laudatory endorsements from prominent people crowding the jacket? In fact, those endorsements may be the most important factor in helping you decide whether or not to buy the book.

The right endorsements add significant value to a book's commercial prospects. If you demonstrate to the publisher upfront that Lee Iacocca is prepared to write a foreword for your business book and that H. Ross Perot is ready to contribute a great blurb, that should be reflected in the advance.

Of course, you don't need only household names backing you up. Writs from people with the right credentials will also be effective—even if they're not famous.

There are many ways to get endorsements—but you must focus on people or organizations relevant to your material. For instance, Iacocca wouldn't be the most appropriate endorsement for a cookbook, but the White House chef would be.

Ask yourself these questions:

- Who do you know?
- Who do your friends know?
- Who do their friends know?

Don't be bashful; seek out and pursue all possible leads. Many noteworthy people are happy to endorse books that they believe in. In many cases, it provides valuable publicity for them, too. The hard part is reaching these candidates and getting them to notice your work. This may, like most endeavors in writing and publishing, require tenacious work—but it will often prove to be well worth the exertion.

Show the publisher all the flattering comments or commitments you've secured when you first submit the proposal. This will establish at the outset that significant people know you and your work, and are willing to vouch for it. This makes a favorable first impression, wins you more serious consideration from the publisher, and enhances your work's perceived value from day one.

CHAPTER 12

What About Fiction?

The Art and Science of Selling Fiction

Fiction and nonfiction work in very different ways. Publishers generally require that most or all of a fiction manuscript be written, or else they won't even consider reading it. This is especially true if you've never had a work of fiction published before.

Unlike nonfiction, fiction requires total upfront speculation by the writer. And the odds that you'll ever get the book published are scary. Nevertheless, countless people invest countless hours and many sleepless nights writing their fiction manuscripts. (If you're reading this chapter, you're probably one of those noble people, or may soon become one.)

Intellectually, these people probably are aware of the tough reality of trying to sell fiction. Fortunately, that knowledge doesn't extinguish their bold efforts. Almost every day, a new novel by a new writer is discovered and scheduled for publication.

Strategies for Selling Your Fiction

Once you have the manuscript finished, it's time to begin the journey to publication. As a first step, you should try to get an agent. A good agent will get your work the necessary access to editors, which is difficult to achieve without an agent. Access won't ensure publication, but nonaccess will ensure nonpublication.

There are many ways to get an agent for fiction. Most agents would like you to follow the protocol of initiating contact by submitting a one-page query letter with a two- to five-page story synopsis. Don't forget to include the self-addressed stamped envelope.

See Chapter 10 on query letters for solid advice about this important step. The synopsis can be organized by chapter or just as an integrated overview. It should serve to capture your entire story in an exceptionally readable, enticing, and lucid style. You want to motivate the agent to request to see some or all of your manuscript.

This synopsis is important because most agents don't want to receive unsolicited manuscripts or chapters. They want control of what comes into their offices—many hefty manuscripts arriving at once can quickly take over office space. An agent once said that if you put two or more manuscripts next to each other, they'll breed like rabbits.

If you decide to (or maybe have to) sell your fiction to a publisher without the benefits of an agent, it would be wise to follow the same protocol. Send your query letter and synopsis to editors first. Unsolicited manuscripts sent to editors are likely to end up in the "slush" room, which can be a lot like being blasted into outer space without a space ship. *The Insider's Guide to Book Editors, Publishers and Literary Agents*, by Jeff Herman (Prima) can help you locate the appropriate agents and editors for your book.

Other details to keep in mind:

- Use attractive, customized stationery, as opposed to unappealing computer paper.
- Personalize *all* correspondence so that your letter does not resemble junk mail.
- Use a good printer. The better it looks, the better you look.
- Send only manuscripts that are double-spaced and in good physical condition.

SECTION TWO

10 Proposals That Sold —And Why

Introduction to Section Two

Here are 10 real, successful, though slightly abridged, nonfiction book proposals accompanied by our critiques. We didn't include sample chapters, press clips, and other collateral materials. While it's invaluable for you to incorporate these materials as part of your total package, presenting them here would have gone beyond the scope of this book.

PROPOSAL I

Cutting the Cord
How to Get Your Adult Children to Grow Up

by Cindy Graves
and
Larry Stockman, Ph.D.

This proposal generated significant interest and was published in hardcover by Contemporary Books under the title *Adult Children Who Won't Grow Up*. It was a selection of Psychology Today Book Club and is currently enjoying a healthy backlisted life as a paperback reprint (Prima Publishing).

This model packs substantial energy and information into a relatively concise presentation. It quickly establishes credibility and creates the invaluable impression that the authors are pros.

In retrospect, the only missing component here is a sample chapter. Since neither author had ever written a book, a strong chapter would have addressed whatever reservations prospective publishers may have had about the authors and may have leveraged a higher advance.

Overview

1. This is a good start for the overview. It uses appropriate imagery to set the stage for the book idea and states a strong thesis.

"If you love your children, give them just two things—give them roots ¹ and give them wings." Sayings similar to this appear on cross-stitched samplers in nurseries across the United States. The ultimate goal of a loving parent is to see their "fledglings" grow strong enough to fly away from the nest and successfully cope with life on their own. In this country, the normal process of growth and development has recently and unexpectedly been thwarted.

2. The supporting data show that research has been undertaken, giving credibility and a statistical base. However, the overview could use a stronger statement of why this problem is an epidemic throughout this particular generation.

Susan Littwin in her recent book *The Postponed Generation: Why* ² *American Youth Are Growing Up Later* (William Morrow, 1986) describes in detail the difficulties of young adults (ages 20-40) in separating themselves from their parents. Psychologists and psychiatrists across the country report an "epidemic"—countless parents coming for assistance with their dependent adult children. In the Houston offices of Human Affairs International, a large mental health counseling center, the staff of 15 counselors estimates that they will handle 2,000 cases (of a total 2,700 cases) involving this problem in 1987 alone.

3. This establishes that there are significant secondary markets for the subject. It would be an appropriate place to make a more direct statement about the primary market, parents who can't get their children to leave the nest.

The problem goes well beyond the 22 million adult children esti- ³ mated by the U.S. Census Bureau to be living at home. It includes children who continually turn to their parents for financial assistance, or who create crisis after crisis to continue an emotional dependency. The financial, emotional, and marital strain on the parents is enormous.

4. Strong reinforcement that the problem is widespread and merits a book on the subject.

The number of young adults who do not live at home, but who are still dependent on their parents is difficult to estimate. But it would not be unreasonable to estimate that at least 40% of the current crop of young adults (20-40 years of age) are excessively dependent. This ⁴ would mean that approximately 36 million young adults are taking longer than any prior generation to sever the ties of adolescence.

5. Responds to the question, "Now that we know the problem, what do we do?" In marketing terms, the authors have created a need and have shown how they will fill it.

Cutting the Cord is a book designed for the parents of these young adults. Facing a problem they never expected, most parents blame themselves and make excuses for their children. This book is ⁵ designed to break the useless guilt trap and allow parents to respond in a way that gently but firmly forces their children "out of the nest." It will be a practical self-help book along the lines of *ToughLove Solutions* by York, York, and Wachtel (Doubleday, 1984). *ToughLove* addressed the difficulties of dealing with "acting out" adolescents. As ⁶

6. By the end of the overview, we have a clear and focused picture of what the book is about and why it's needed.

ToughLove has spawned support groups across the nation and another book (*ToughLove: A Self-Help Manual*), we expect *Cutting the Cord* to have the same potential market.

Market Analysis

7 Phyllis Feuerstein and Carol Roberts's book, *The Not-So-Empty Nest: How to Live With Your Kids After They've Lived Someplace Else* (Follett, 1981), is no longer in print, but it marks the first recognition of the trend of delayed maturity. This book gave advice to parents on how to survive the period of time when young adults come back home—not on how to get them to stop being dependent. It addresses all the "needs" of the adult child, but not the fundamental maladjustment. Since this only amplifies the guilt of the parent, the book was of no real help to the readers most likely to buy it.

8 There are several books currently on the market in this general area, but none is a self-help manual for parents designed to deal with the larger picture—the adult child who is dependent but may not live 9 at home. Littwin's book *The Postponed Generation* shows the enormity of the problem, but does not offer any advice to parents dealing with it on a daily basis.

Released in October were two more books dealing with the extended childhood of many of today's young adults. One is a book along the line of *Passages*, and is intended for the young adults (*"Grown-Ups": A Generation in Search of Adulthood*, Putnam, 1987). This book is clearly not competing for our target audience.

The second book is titled *Boomerang Kids* and is written by two psychologists, J.D. Okimoto and P.J. Stegall (Little, Brown, 1987). *Boomerang Kids*, however, has as its primary emphasis kids who come home to live, not the greater problem of extended dependency in all its varied forms. In addition, its emphasis is clearly on parents adjusting to the trials of children coming home again—not on ending the dependency.

10 Magazines have carried stories on this problem (*Woman's Day*, July 7, 1987; and *Time*, May 4, 1987), and Regis Philbin recently addressed the issue on his show. The subject is highly topical, and *Cutting the Cord* is the book to fill the need for a self-help book that deals with the whole problem—not just a piece of it. But we cannot be alone in recognizing the opportunity. Rapid action will be needed to be the first such book on the shelves.

---

7. Incorporates competition and tackles it head on. Gives very concrete and specific distinguishing factors showing the authors took the time to do their research.

8. Distinguishing factors that reinforce the importance of the proposed book. The authors define the very specific purpose of this book in contrast to what already exists on the market.

9. With the phrase "enormity of the problem," the authors create an urgency that benefits this type of subject.

10. Shows there is an immediate market, which may motivate the editor to make a rapid decision and speed the process. However, the topical nature of this book proposal could work against it, as a market becomes saturated very quickly. It might have been better to make a positive statement that the authors are ahead of the trend rather than planting the seed that they "cannot be alone..."

11. This proposal should include a marketing section that features ideas for where the book can be placed as well as ideas for promotion.

12. This is good, stating clearly and concisely what the book will do. The authors come across as logical and thorough.

13. This shows the best of all worlds: (a) professional credentials, (b) personal experience, and (c) ability to write.

14. Can't ask for much more than this. The credentials (about the author) section focuses on the expertise of the lead author, who must show credibility to give substance to a book of this kind. The only additional credentials, which would have made our job almost too easy, would have been celebrity status, extensive media/public speaking experience, and at least one previously published book.

15. The coauthor establishes solid and relevant credentials. However,

Our Approach   11

We plan to write a 50,000-word book in simple terminology targeted toward the parents of adult dependent children. We will begin with an explanation of the problem and how healthy dependency and unhealthy dependency are different. This will be followed by a discussion of those feelings that tend to paralyze parents: guilt, embarrassment, confusion, the need to control, and so on. The viewpoints of parents and young adults enmeshed in this difficulty will be quoted 12 to demonstrate that the reader is not alone in this problem, and to give some perspective on the feelings of the dependent child. We will explain how parental behavior can either allow the situation to continue or work to correct it.

The book will then move to practical advice, itemizing typical situations and ways to respond. Details from various actual cases will be brought in to illustrate significant points. The reader will finish the book feeling that he/she now has some ideas to apply to his or her particular situation.

Credentials   13

As a writing team, we bring writing expertise as well as the perspectives of counselor and parent to this project.

Larry Stockman, Ph.D., has been involved in the counseling field since 1961. He is currently the manager of the Houston office of Human Affairs International (a counseling firm). He supervises 15 counselors and manages the Exxon Corporation Employee Health 14 Advisory Program. He has personally been involved in counseling at least 500 families with adult child extended dependency problems, and is responsible for overseeing approximately 2,000 such cases at HAI in 1987 alone.

In addition to his counseling background, Larry has five graduate degrees to his credit, as well as an extensive list of university and government publications. Larry has traveled extensively, living and working in such remote places as Capachica, Peru. He has developed a great sensitivity to the influences of various cultures and religions on human behavior, and is uniquely qualified to advise American parents on this unusual phenomenon of extended dependency.

Cindy Graves, a longtime writer, received her undergraduate 15 degree in English, magna cum laude, from Duke University. She received her master's degree in political science from Duke one year later with a 3.8 GPA. Presently working as an employee-relations

[15] supervisor for a Fortune 500 company, Cindy has two stepdaughters ages 19 and 21. The older daughter's dependency problem has brought Cindy closely in contact with the issue of delayed adulthood. In addition, similar problems with other members of her immediate family caused her to research this issue and discover the vast number of parents struggling with the same problem. Cindy offers not only her writing experience to this project, but also her perspective as a parent trying to cope with the endlessly varied manifestations of this emotionally draining problem. She is very conscious of the ways a child can remain dependent while not living at home, and the impact that dependency has on other family members and on the parents' marriage.

[16] # Outline
Chapter 1: Healthy and Unhealthy Dependency
[17] Jane Goodall, in her multigenerational observations of a tribe of chimpanzees in Africa, observed one dysfunctional family unit that surprised all animal behaviorists. Documented in her book *In the Shadow of Man*, and later in a television documentary, were Flo, an elderly female, and her second-to-last child, a son named Flint. When her last child was born, Flo was too weak to force Flint from the nest they had shared for his first two years of life. Flint was stubborn and strong and remained dependent until Flo's death several years later. Following Flo's death, Flint refused to eat or to interact with the other chimps. Eventually he passed away, unwilling to take care of himself.

This story of extended chimpanzee childhood has direct parallels in human behavior. But the lines between healthy and unhealthy [18] dependency are rarely so clear. This chapter will help the reader understand the difference, using both narrative explanation and a self-diagnostic test.

To set the stage, healthy dependency will be explained. Such [19] ideal parenting is called "egalitarian"—or "teaching self-dependency and trust." The normal development of a child into an adult will also be outlined. But how does a parent know when they are not being "egalitarian" or the child is not developing normally? The authors will explain three common parental behavior traps: (1) authoritarian behavior, demanding "blind" obedience; (2) permissive/insecure behavior, allowing almost all behavior out of fear of loss of the child's affection; and (3) overprotective behavior, meddling in all the child's affairs.

though she identifies herself as a writer, we don't see any documentation for that. It might be better not to draw attention to writing experience unless it can be substantiated. The proposal is written well enough to show her ability to complete the project effectively, but any good publication credits or clippings should be included to strengthen the package.

16. The authors should have included a separate table of contents so the publisher could see an overview of the book's structure.

17. This is a very compelling beginning to the chapter summaries—the absorbing anecdote sets the tone for the book. The chapter summaries include enough substance to show both style and direction, giving the publisher a clear picture of what to expect.

18. This offers a program aspect to the book, which is very useful in self-help projects. This type of information lends itself to promotion and is a logical first step.

19. The outline contains more detailed information than some proposals do. This is a good idea for a self-help book because publishers and writers run a risk if the book isn't well focused.

The authors continue to demonstrate that they have a strong handle on the dynamics of this phenomenon.

20. This quiz, a useful and potentially valuable bonus, is a good idea for media exposure. It helps compensate for the lack of a formal marketing or promotions section.

From the other side of the coin, how does a parent know when a child's dependency is "abnormal"? What is the difference between calling for advice and calling to get Mommy or Daddy to decide everything from which bank to use to what type of toaster to buy? When is it not reasonable for a child to expect financial assistance anymore? The authors will explain several types of typical dependency behavior.

The chapter will conclude with a quiz which will allow the [20] reader to evaluate his/her own behavior and that of the child. A scoring system will allow the reader to determine the severity of the dependency problem. (This quiz will also be designed for easy resale to magazines.)

Chapter 2: Is It My Fault?

The endless parental nightmare—was it something I did? The Judeo-Christian culture is quick to blame the parents for the failings of the child. Yet few are the psychologists or behaviorists who would say that all behavior is the result of parental training. Genetics, instinct, or some other metaphysical influence may be equally important. But the nature/nurture argument is for philosophers, not parents coping with a problem.

The authors will explain that there are other factors that go into a child's behavior, but regardless of the cause, searching for blame only wastes energy. What parents need is a way to respond now. Time can be given later to the philosophical questions.

The reader will be shown how to recognize unhealthy "guilt trips" when they are self-inflicted, or inflicted by others. Once identified, the reader can then use the steps outlined to break the paralyzing hold of such guilt and move on to positive thought and action.

The final section of this chapter will specifically address the greatest user of parental guilt: the child. A child learns at a very early age how to gain reactions from its parents. The toughest part for the parents is learning to stop their ingrained reactions, thereby thwarting the adult child's manipulation. This is essential if the parent is to stop anguishing over the problem at hand, and act on it instead. Specific advice will show parents how to respond to statements such as: "Well, if we hadn't moved so much I'd be more settled by now."

Chapter 3: Encouraging the Problem

Both parents and adult children have needs that can cause them to subconsciously continue an extended dependency. Until those drives are recognized and defused, the subconscious needs will sabotage the best conscious intent to change things. This chapter will show the parent how to recognize those drives in their own situation and work to eliminate them. The following specific parental desires will be addressed:

- "My kids should have it easier than I did."
- "Money can make up for the time I didn't spend with my kid."
- "My kids are a reflection of my success—what will the neighbors think if they don't succeed?"
- "I am the parent; I am in control. I will make my child meet my expectations."
- "My primary role in life is as a parent. I am nothing without that" (empty-nest fears).
- "If we don't have the child to distract us, my spouse and I will have to look at our marriage for the first time in years."
- "But what if something bad happens to my 'baby?'" (overprotectiveness).
- "But if I refuse the requests, my child might not come see me anymore."

Excerpts from interviews with parents will be included to give real-life dimension to these feelings.

The authors will show how unrealistic and unhealthy these needs or fears are and show parents constructive ways to work out of their own "codependency."

Chapter 4: What's in It for Johnny/Mary?

Kids have their own reasons for wanting to continue the dependency, some of which may be quite surprising to parents. Understanding the motives that may be inspiring the reader's child will help that reader determine the best way to defuse his or her manipulative behaviors. This chapter will itemize the motives, which may not be conscious, that keep the child coming back again and again.

- Inability to cope with parents' divorce (children who may want their divorced parents to get back together again).
- Insecurity (children—particularly if adopted—may manipulate their parents and create crises to "prove" they are loved).
- Laziness.
- Fear of responsibility.
- Fear of failure as an adult/provider/employee/etc.
- Fear/dislike of independence (decisions were always made for them when they were younger).

21

21. This section is strong because it promises parents a method for discovering the hidden causes, devoid of judgment. When writing this type of book, keep in mind the anxiety levels your readers can handle as you illuminate all of their mistakes. This would be a good place to include an example of how the authors intend to integrate interviews into the text.

- Peer pressure (everyone else is getting money from their parents).
- "Mom and Dad owe it to me" (the entitlement syndrome—or, "what's yours is mine and what's mine is mine").
- "Mom and Dad can afford it."
- Anger/revenge for perceived injustices.
- Materialistic expectations that cannot be met immediately "on the outside."
- Enjoyment of dependency.

This chapter is not designed to make the parent feel that if they "only understood" their child's problem and could "communicate better" it would all go away. Chances are excellent that the adult child has no idea what his/her motives are. But even if he did, talk will not change behavior. Parents will have to act and react differently than they have in the past to evoke different behaviors in the child, leading, it is hoped, to growth in his or her personality. But that is a separate question, one outside the scope of this book. The authors' goal is to get parents out of the philosophical realm and to deal with the here and now. The motives of the child are useful to understand only insofar as they advise the parent how to behave, or not to behave, in the present.

Chapter 4 will include excerpts of interviews with dependent young adults. The language and arguments they use will probably sound familiar to the reader. Chapters 5 through 9 will then deal with specific common situations and how to address them based on case studies.

22. Here's another reinforcement that the book will be practical and program oriented. Philosophical books have their place, but the commercial market looks for tangible information that can easily be conveyed to the lay reader.

23. The authors should have given at least one example of a dynamic case study.

Chapters 5-8: Case Studies   23
Chapters 5 through 8 will illustrate common dependency/codependency situations using case studies. The case studies selected will be those considered representative of the 1,000 client cases handled by Human Affairs International in 1987. Each case study will involve in-depth interviews with the clients. The reader will be given a brief history of the situation and sample comments from the parents and the dependent child. These will let the readers know that they are not alone in their feelings and problems. In those cases in which they can see themselves or their child, it will give them a more objective view of the unhealthy dependency behaviors being exhibited.

Chapter 5 will address the authoritarian parent and submissive child pattern. Chapter 6 will demonstrate a permissive/insecure parent and the child who takes advantage of that weakness. Chapter 7 deals with the overprotective parent and fearful child. Chapter 8 confronts the problem of chemically dependent children (drug addicts, alcoholics) and the way they tie their parents into codependency.

Chapter 9: Now What Do I Do?

Now that the reader has some idea of the nature of the adult child's dependency behavior, and his or her own codependency, what can the reader do to end the cycle? This chapter will give specific advice to parents—first on how to stop participating in the problem. "What do I say when Johnny calls and asks me for money?" "What do I do when Mary drops by unannounced with her laundry?" These common, everyday problems will be addressed in terms that leave the reader feeling as though he or she has some concrete ideas on how to respond to his or her own particular situation.

Second, the authors will give advice on how to encourage the child to seek different behaviors, and reward him/her when they appear. When the child makes a decision on his/her own, what should the parent say? If Johnny decides to rent an apartment beyond his means, but takes on a second job to do it, should anything be said? Learning to reinforce the stumbling efforts to grow into adulthood takes time.

In the final portion of this chapter, advice will be offered regarding the formation of support groups. Sometimes even the strongest wills can falter when faced with the skillful manipulations of a son or daughter. Someone in a similar situation can provide invaluable support. Just knowing that others are struggling as well is sometimes all the support that is needed. But in some cases, professional assistance may be necessary. The reader will be told how to know when it's time to seek help from a professional counselor, and be given a few tips on selecting one.

* * * * *

The reader will finish the book with valuable tools to assist in working out the problem with his/her child: how to get friends to help when needed and when to turn to professionals for assistance. Most importantly, however, the reader will know that he/she is not alone—that this is not a problem that should be hidden or denied, or one that should cause shame. The reader should feel some of the burden of guilt lifted and feel hopeful that a solution to the problem can be found.

24. This is a confident and optimistic closing. Readers often need to feel some hopefulness at the end of a provocative book.

PROPOSAL 2

How to Get Clients
An Easy and Practical Program to Build Your Business

by
Jeff Slutsky
with
Marc Slutsky

Several editors made offers on this proposal, which was sold to Warner Books. It was published as a how-to popular business book in a quality paperback format with the same main title, *How to Get Clients*.

The proposal is well organized and captures the author's expertise and special self-marketing skills, projecting energy, enthusiasm, and a nonintimidating "you can do this, too" approach.

The primary obstacle here was that there were many good books on the subject already in print. The authors didn't include a sample chapter, but in this case it didn't matter. The outline was well done, and the principal author had written two other commercially successful books.

1. This is what overviews are all about. In one tight paragraph, the authors completely describe what the book will do for the reader and show the publisher that there's a market for it. This paragraph reflects confidence and the ability to deliver.

What's *How to Get Clients* About?

How to Get Clients teaches and guides professionals and those responsible for marketing service-oriented businesses on how to build their client base. With this book the reader learns every aspect and skill needed to build a successful service business by getting clients who pay big fees. The readers discover how to identify or create their special market niche, how to initially contact the potential client, gather needed information about the client, make the presentation designed to get a positive decision, and even how to dominate the marketplace in their area. With consolidation, takeovers, restructuring, and mergers of major service organizations including the big eight (now big six) accounting firms, advertising agencies, law firms, insurance and financial institutions and a host of others, hundreds of thousands of professionals have gone on their own or have joined smaller organizations. They must learn how to get clients to survive. This book is the answer to their survival.

2. While it's unusual to place the table of contents so early in the proposal, it's perfectly acceptable. By doing so here, the author quickly delivers the program aspect of the book. Substance put this proposal over the top.

Each chapter title is strong and effective. A publisher looking at this table of contents can visualize exactly how the book will be structured. This shows good organization and a logical progression of the material.

Table of Contents

Introduction

Chapter 1: Who Are Your Potential Clients and Why Do You Want Them

Chapter 2: How to Discover and Develop Your Unique Market Niche

Chapter 3: 14 Ways to Establish Credibility That Make Clients Take Notice

Chapter 4: How to Make an Effective First Contact and Avoiding Wasting Your Time

Chapter 5: How to Dominate Your Marketplace Without Spending a Fortune

Chapter 6: 10 Techniques for Avoiding Fee Shopping

Chapter 7: When Advertising Makes Sense and How to Do It for Less

Chapter 8: The Value of Free Publicity and How to Get It

Chapter 9: How to Communicate Persuasively to Get a "Yes"

Chapter 10: Proposals and Presentations: 5 Rules for Results

3. This introduction may not have been necessary because it seems to repeat information from the overview.

Introduction

How to Get Clients is a unique and complete marketing guide specifically written to help professionals develop a larger and more profitable client base. Most professionals have little or no marketing experience, especially in the complex and confusing area of selling services to new prospective buyers. Yet there are hundreds of thousands of professionals in numerous areas that have to get more clients to pay higher fees for their services if they are to survive in the difficult times ahead.

4   The service economy is increasingly more competitive. As a result large companies are restructuring, merging, and consolidating, leaving hundreds of thousands of highly skilled professionals to fend for themselves. Their only alternative is to go out on their own or team up with others in the same situation. While they are perfectly competent in their specific areas, they now have to take on new responsibilities. The most important of which is to get new clients so they can pay their bills. It's a matter of survival.

4. This shows a growing need for the material.

5 # Who Buys *How to Get Clients* and Why?

Target Audience—The strongest target group most likely to buy this book is professionals who have gone out on their own or are given the responsibility of client acquisition in their present organization. It is also "must" reading for any aggressive corporate person who wants to climb the corporate ladder of any service organization because, while any trained professional can do the work for clients, it's the partners and future partners who actually bring the clients into the firm. Just a few service areas that use this information include:

5. This effective market section is focused and credible even without the reinforcement of statistics from respected publications.

Accounting/CPAs/Tax
Advertising/Public Relations
Architectural/Contracting
Business Consulting
Computer/Telecommunications
Finance
Franchising
Fund Raising

Insurance
Investments/Brokers/CICs
Law Firms/Legal
Manufacturing/Wholesaling
Medical/Dental/Hospitals
Research/Information
Retrieval

6   For example, in a recent issue of *Business Week*, an article entitled, "For Law Firms, It's Dog v. Dog Out There"[1] stressed how the legal profession is becoming increasingly competitive. A sidebar article went on further to stress the need for sales and marketing. The article, entitled, "The Latest Law Course: Marketing 101"[2], went on to say:

6. The quotations cited are on target and offer a solid foundation for the author's marketing claims.

> For the lawyers, it represents a bold new step into the world of competitive business. Traditionally they had shunned overt marketing efforts because of ethical restrictions and professional biases. But the rules have eased. **In today's saturated legal market, firms are looking for every advantage they can find.**

---

[1] *Business Week*, August 6, 1990. (Legal Affairs Section) "For Law Firms, It's Dog v. Dog Out There" by Michael Galen with Tim Smart and Geoff Smith and Keith Hammonds.

[2] *Business Week*, August 6, 1990. "The Latest Law Course: Marketing 101" by Michael Galen. Pg 58.

Take a look at another high-end profession where sales and marketing is just now becoming a major part of the practice. The first item of the "Business Bulletin"[3] on the front page of the *Wall Street Journal* recently had the following:

> More lawsuits and the S&L crisis cause firms to take steps against exposure. The American Institute of CPAs tightens its membership rules. A national survey finds eight of 10 midsize accounting firms restrict services and 56% won't take clients considered 'high-risk.'

This means that with less clients to choose from, accounting firms are becoming more aggressive in going after the business they do want. For the first time, sales and marketing is becoming a vital part of a successful CPA firm.

Anyone who needs to have clients to pay the bills needs this book. It makes no difference whether it's a branch office of AT&T or IBM or a single consultant with a part-time secretary, this book gives field-proven techniques needed to master the art of getting clients. **7**

Buyers' Benefits with *How to Get Clients* **8**

1) Complete step-by-step program easily adaptable to any service organization.
2) Most effective, up-to-date, proven client acquisition techniques.
3) Easy to learn and use for *non*sales or *non*marketing people.
4) Ideas that are easily absorbed in the operation of the company.
5) Negates the need for expensive and perhaps ineffective outside marketing and sales specialists.
6) Puts the reader in control of his or her own destiny.
7) Features nine ways for the reader to get potential clients to initiate the contact which saves time and puts the reader at a great advantage when negotiating fees.
8) Ideas and techniques are fun to read and easy to understand.

Publisher's Benefits **9**

1) **A Proven Program**—You market a client acquisition book using ideas with a proven track record in the field, not only by the author himself, but by many of his clients and associates. The concepts get results, which makes the book a popular back-list title that is sure to bring you strong sales for years to come.

---

[3] *The Wall Street Journal,* "Business Bulletin," August 23, 1990, Pg 1.   **10**

7. The authors identify the key market segments likely to be attracted to the book, extending the market beyond the obvious and showing broad potential. "Field-proven techniques" are always great.

8. It was smart to itemize these benefits in a separate category.

9. Itemizing the publisher's potential benefits in this way was a creative and bold move. But if you try it, make sure not to fill it with fluff, overzealousness, or signs of major egotism.

10. Strong source materials bolster the author's case.

2) **Expandable**—This book, once proven successful, lends itself to sequels and special editions geared for a specific group which pays double or triple retail for access to this information.

3) **Writing Track Record**—The author has three successful published books and one published audio album to date as well as several self-published projects including video and audio.

4) **Promotional Track Record**—The author delivers close to a hundred speeches a year to prominent associations and corporations, giving tremendous visibility for this book. The associations include the American Booksellers with additional exposure in *Publisher's Weekly*.

What's My Background?

My background and abilities are ideally suited to make *How to Get Clients* a big success. My strengths, as I see them, are threefold:

1) *Solid professional credentials and practical experience*—I founded the Retail Marketing Institute over ten years ago after leaving an advertising agency for which I was promoted to Vice President at age 23. With a background in both traditional advertising and public relations I began to develop, discover, and adapt ways of using results-oriented, low-cost marketing to get us clients.

Over the past ten years, I have worked with many organizations of various sizes to develop their client acquisition program. While the material in *How to Get Clients* is simple and easily adaptable, it is based on actual success stories. There are no theories here, only proven programs that work and will work for the reader.

I know it works because I use it for my organization and my clients. I've also gathered many other ideas, stories, and strategies from the people that made them work. All of this has been presented in workshops and speeches hundreds upon hundreds of times all over the country and around the world. I have worked with organizations as large as AT&T, American Express, Firestone, Honda, CBS Records, Ramada Inns, Hilton, McDonald's, the city of Dallas, the State of Arkansas, and the country of India! I have also worked with organizations as small as Versatile Investments, Steven Trotter's Legal Clinic, Dr. Donald Pritt, Podiatrist, and Silvan Krel, CPA. The one thing they have in common is that they've paid thousands of dollars for this information.

Marc Slutsky started working part time with me about five years ago and then came on board full time three years ago. He has an education background with a specialty in special education.

11. "About the Author" sections are usually written in the third person. Some people find it easier to blow their own horn without using "I." In this case, first person is highly effective. The principal author makes a strong statement that amplifies his very impressive background without sounding arrogant.

12. This "About the Author" section's strength is that is doesn't miss an opportunity to persuade the publisher about the merits of the book. You don't need to list all of your accomplishments since kindergarten. Publishers are more impressed with credentials relevant to the potential success of your book.

Many of the techniques he used to train his students have been [12] incorporated into our program to make it as easy as possible for a business professional to learn and use these ideas.

This past July I was awarded the CSP (Certified Speaking Professional) designation by the National Speakers Association. This title is held by less than 5% of the NSA membership.

2) *A publishing track record*—To have a good idea is one thing; to turn it into a book is another. I know I can turn *How To Get Clients* into a great selling book because I have written three books to date that are. They are *Streetfighting: Low Cost Advertising & Marketing For Your Business, Street Smart Marketin,g* and *The 33 Secrets Of Street Smart Tele-Selling.*

Streetfighting (Prentice Hall, 1984)—After a couple of years I acquired the rights and the negs and now self-publish it. In one year, I personally sold out the remainder of the first printing, some 3400 copies in hard cover after raising the price from $18 to $25. It was picked up by the Adweek Book Club and the Entrepreneur Magazine Book Club as well as promoted by many trade organizations to their members. It is a consistent seller for these groups.

13. It's a smart move for the author to bring attention to his previous books, and to highlight his proven ability to help sell substantial copies. Publishers like it when a prospective author with a good project has been successfully published in the recent past.

The book is now in its sixth printing. With a newly designed [13] dust cover and a new list price of $30, sales are still going strong with close to 50,000 copies sold to date. *Streetfighting* is an interesting, practical, and clever book which is the furthest thing from a text book that you would ever read. It now enjoys the tremendous credibility of being recognized by many major universities and is required reading in many business schools and entrepreneur classes, including Indiana University, Northwestern, and the University of Deudlin in New Zealand.

Since we sell *Streetfighting* ourselves, we know where people hear about it. Most of our book sales are referrals. Arby's received one promotional copy then ordered 150 more at full price, and we're still getting follow up orders to this day. Chick-fil-A, a fast food operation in Atlanta, ordered 500 copies and now buys *Street Smart Marketing* in quantity direct from the publisher as required reading for every single employee. Amoco Oil, Honda, H & R Block, U-Haul, Greyhound, Photo Marketing Institute, and the Retail Bakers Association are other examples of companies consistently ordering in quantity. Firestone bought 1100 copies for each of their retail dealers, and Baskin Robbins bought 3200 copies in a special run for each of their franchisees.

Street Smart Marketing (John Wiley & Sons, 1989)—While *Streetfighting* is successful, *Street Smart Marketing* targets a much larger and more profitable market. The former was geared toward small independent businesses. This newer book takes those same ideas, combined with four more years of new ideas, and gears them to the profitable corporate environment.

Street Smart Tele-Selling: The 33 Secrets (Prentice Hall, 1990) was just released. It's geared for the tens of thousands of corporations and businesses that need to sell to the business community. Prentice Hall also produced an audio cassette album with workbook under the same title. The book features a forward by Robert L. Shook.

My first three books prove I can write in an easy-to-understand and very entertaining style, packed with useful ideas.

3) *A wealth of media exposure and experience*—When it comes to promotion and marketing, I practice what I preach. Not only do you get a quality manuscript, but you also get an author who is promotable and is a promoter. I know how to take advantage of opportunity and turn it into sales.

I'm a performer and do extremely well in an interview situation. In addition to the national publications in which I've been featured, including the *Wall Street Journal, INC* Magazine, *USA Today,* and *Success,* I've also received a great deal of exposure from dailies including the Chicago *Tribune,* Chicago *Sun Times,* San Francisco *Chronicle,* and a host of others. I've been on hundreds of radio and TV shows including CNN, *Nation's Business* on ESPN, WFYR Chicago, WMCA New York, and KMPC in Los Angeles and was on KCBS in San Francisco four times.

One of the most exciting bits of exposure was when I was asked to be a featured speaker at the American Booksellers Association convention this year. As a result, *Publishers Weekly* did a feature story about me and my books, and ABA has invited me back for next year's convention in New York. In addition, I now am a presenter on a regular basis for the National Speakers Association. This is a trade association of some 3500 professional speakers who collectively reach millions of business people every year. Only a small percentage of our membership is invited to present programs to its members, and I do so on a regular basis. As a result, hundreds of speakers quote from my books, creating additional demand for them.

14

14. This shows verve and creativity. The principal author has demonstrated genuine confidence throughout the proposal, peppered with the facts to support his claims.

This author's promotions credentials are highly impressive. You can work to build your resume, as he has—but don't overlook anything you already have in your favor. This author is affiliated with organizations that enhance his status in the field, and show he has the respect of colleagues.

Delivery of the Book

The book will be about 50,000 words plus illustrations and charts. There will be 10 chapters, each of which includes several subheadings. The complete manuscript will be delivered February 15, 1991. I write with WordPerfect 5.1, and the diskette will also be made available if you so request.

Chapter Summaries

Chapter 1: Who Are Your Potential Clients and Why Do You Want Them?

Before you can begin to go after new clients you have to determine what type of clients you really want. This can be the most important step because often-times professionals make an effort to go after clients only to find out years later that they've pigeonholed themselves into a segment of the marketplace that is not very profitable.

The first step is to conduct a simple "internal capabilities audit" to see what your company's strengths and weaknesses are. By playing to your strengths and avoiding weak areas you'll be able to compete on a much stronger footing than your competitors.

You also have to develop some simple guidelines for your account acquisition program that tell you when to go forward and when to "dump out" of an effort. Developing ways for looking for "red flags" or potential trouble areas are critical at this stage before you invest too much of your time or money in getting the client. A few "red flags" include how fast they pay their bills, turnover of similar services, turnover of their personnel, etc.

In this chapter you learn:

1) How to identify the profitable clients from the ones that only talk a [15] good game yet waste your time and eventually lose you money.
2) The 10 steps for determining just how profitable a client will be in the short term.
3) Three steps for determining the long-term value of this client.
4) Why some clients have a need to exaggerate their value to you and how to avoid this.
5) How to determine residual value of a client beyond fees.
6) The 17 red flags to watch out for in determining if a client is going to be more trouble than he's worth.
7) How to develop a plan for guaranteeing that your client base is complementary and avoids duplication of effort.

15. This chapter-by-chapter outline is complete, yet not bogged down with too much copy. The authors start with a reflection of the book's voice, and list the chapter highlights clearly and concisely. It's very effective to itemize the various "missions" of each chapter like this. This outline gives the impression that there won't be any hot-air filler in this book.

Chapter 2: How to Discover and Develop Your Unique Market Niche

After you've determined which types of clients are best for your situation, you need to go one step further and ascertain your market niche. This is a critical step because it is a major factor that determines your fee levels. Generally, the more you are a specialist in a given area, the higher the fees. But you have to be careful not to pick a market that is limited in any way.

Your niche is governed by two factors: 1) the type of service you provide and 2) where you provide it. If you have a geographical territory, that in itself is a partial niche. A computer consultant, for example may specialize in putting in complete systems for the medical profession and may further limit the niche by staying within a 100 mile radius from his home office. To expand, you then have three choices: expand your territory (which could have its downside); expand your market (find additional niches), which forces you into areas that you may not have the same level of expertise; and/or provide more services to an existing niche, which also challenges your expertise.

In this chapter, you learn:

1) How to discover the most profitable niche for you.
2) When it's time to expand and how to do it.
3) The five factors for determining when you're spreading yourself too thin and in danger of losing it all.
4) How to work your niche to maximize fees.
5) How to select a niche based on ease of marketability.
6) When to consider switching your niche and how to do it.
7) How to expand by offering new services to existing clients without losing credibility.
8) An overview of dominating your niche and keeping the competition at bay.

Chapter 3: 14 Ways to Establish Credibility That Make Clients Take Notice

Credibility is the key to not only getting clients to hire you but getting them to pay top dollar for your services. How you subtly "toot your own horn" is a major factor in getting the business by winning over the client. There are many ways in which you can get a client to "perceive" your credibility and feeling comfortable paying you a premium for your services.

In this chapter you learn:

1) What credibility is and how it directly factors into your fee level.
2) The power of the client testimonial and how to get it.
3) How the right publicity can establish you as an expert in your field.
4) When writing a book is appropriate and how to do it without really writing it yourself.
5) Identifying your past "hidden" activities that help develop your credibility even further.
6) How to put all your credibility elements together to create additional credibility.
7) How to effectively yet subtly use lack of credibility to give you an edge against the competition.
8) How to identify which elements of credibility are the "hot buttons" for your potential client and how to use them to your advantage.

Chapter 4: How to Make an Effective First Contact and Avoiding Wasting Your Time

The first contact is critical because you only get one opportunity to make a good first impression. That's why the first contact is often one that is not even noticeable by your potential client. You have to do your homework first. There's a plethora of information that can be gathered by phone from non decision makers that helps you greatly when you're ready to "engage." Once you do "engage" there is no turning back. It's close or be killed. You must handle this first encounter with all your options available to you for maximum maneuverability.

In this chapter you learn:

1) What valuable information you need before you "engage" and how to get it without exposing your position.
2) How to know when you're ready for your first encounter.
3) Why you need to use a "fact gathering" mission or "reconnaissance" mission before you're ready to make your major pitch.
4) How to structure fact gathering so that you position yourself for a "no-fail" return visit.
5) When the "dog and pony" show is more of a distraction than help and how to avoid its pitfalls.
6) The magic elements that every potential client wants to know.
7) How to get commitment from your client by presentation's end.
8) Five ways to get your client to pay for your research and presentation.

Chapter 5: How to Dominate Your Marketplace without Spending a Fortune

There are many ways a skilled professional can achieve a leading market position and make it difficult for competition to move in on your territory. It takes thought and effort but with a carefully planned program, you can easily dominate your "turf."

In this chapter you learn:

1) How to determine if your marketplace already has a leader and just how strong that position really is.
2) Seven ways to shut out your competition.
3) How to use trade journals or local news media to your advantage.
4) The power of public speaking in creating your leadership position.
5) How to work with a trade association.
6) How to avoid spending much time and money working with trade associations.
7) How to effectively use your printed support material, articles, newsletters, books, tapes, speeches, and other items to secure and maintain leadership position.
8) Why the leadership position allows you to get 10-100% higher fees for the same work as your nearest competitor.

Chapter 6: 10 Techniques for Avoiding Fee Shopping

When selling a service it is often common for clients to negotiate your fees heavily, playing your competition against you for the best price. Nobody wins at this kind of game and you need to avoid it completely. Selling on price is the weakest position you can take, especially in a competitive situation. You must build "value" for your services and help the client find solutions to problems, not just buy your services.

In this chapter you learn:

1) How to avoid fee shopping before it becomes an issue.
2) How to deal with the "price" issue when it becomes a major objection.
3) When to fight and when to flee.
4) What other problems arise later on in the client relationship when price is the major consideration in hiring you.
5) Ten ways to build high value to justify your price.
6) How to negotiate lower fees when appropriate without losing fee credibility.
7) How and when to add services that the client needs that also add extra profit to your bottom line.

Chapter 7: When Advertising Makes Sense and How to Do It for Less

Service organizations often spend fortunes on advertising, most of which is wasted. There is a time and a place to advertise but you have to know all the basics or you'll end up going under supporting your advertising. You also need to know that the only thing advertising can do is perhaps create some interest and get a potential client to contact you. What you do with that contact really determines the value of your advertising. Advertising itself does not sell clients—you do.

In this chapter you learn:

1) Which media makes the most sense and why.
2) How to negotiate with media to save money and get better results.
3) What to say in your ad so that only qualified potential clients call you.
4) How to follow up an ad so you convert the interested client into a paying client.
5) How to track the results of your advertising.
6) When to consider direct mail, telemarketing, trade journals, yellow pages, etc., and how to use them for less money.
7) How to look for opportunities to barter with the media and not get stung.
8) The proper use of 800 numbers, computer dialing machines, marketing software, and business reply cards.
9) Three ways you can use a two-step process.

Chapter 8: The Value of Free Publicity and How to Get It

One of the best ways to support your business is with free publicity. It does many different things for you and has been mentioned briefly in previous chapters. Now it's time to get it in detail and put this tremendous tool to work for you.

You can't depend on publicity entirely, yet it makes a great supplement to your regular account acquisition program.

In this chapter you learn:

1) How to approach the news media so they want to do your story.
2) How to leverage your publicity long after the item has run.
3) How to handle the interview so clients know how to get in touch with you.
4) Five things to avoid when talking to the media.
5) How to handle negative publicity and why there is no such thing as "off the record."

6) When enough is enough and when too much is harmful.
7) How to determine which media is best for you and which is a waste of your time.
8) Why and when it's good for your business when you're just stroking your own ego.

Chapter 9: How to Communicate Persuasively to Get a "Yes"

The key to your success in getting clients is your ability to communicate persuasively to the prospective client. They have to understand the value of what you have to offer with the same intensity that you do. Selling is not a negative thing. It often brings to mind used car salesmen in polyester sport coats selling lemons to unsuspecting buyers. That's unfortunate. Selling in the 90s is much more. It's a means of helping your prospective client understand how you are going to solve the problem and why they should be happy to pay top dollar.

In this chapter you learn:

1) How to get past the gatekeeper, the person who can't say "yes" but can say "no."
2) How to know when you're talking with the decision maker and why you shouldn't waste your time with others.
3) How to control the conversation by asking questions.
4) How to use the "echo" in fact gathering and discovering client hot buttons.
5) Understanding the painful process of decision making and working it to your advantage.
6) How to properly diagnose your clients' problems and then perform a "cashectomy."
7) How to turn a conversation around after you're on the defensive.
8) When it's time to get the commitment and how to identify client buying signals.

Chapter 10: Proposals and Presentations: Five Rules for Results

The final stage is preparing and presenting the proposal. This should actually be the easy part if all the other stages were followed properly. Yet many things can still happen. To make sure there are no surprises, you have the client help you prepare the proposal. In this way they know exactly what they're getting. No surprises. Furthermore, a client is more likely to buy into a program in which they were involved.

In this chapter you learn:

1) How to get your client involved in the development of the proposal.
2) When it is appropriate to charge a fee for your proposal and how to use your "needs analysis" as a fee generator.
3) How to develop a proposal that is geared for what the client likes and not what you like.
4) How to balance the written proposal with the live presentation.
5) Why a "dog and pony" doesn't get the client.
6) How to structure the numbers so that you have maximum flexibility when it comes down to final negotiations.
7) How to avoid a competitive bid situation and why you'll always lose if you don't.
8) The "one bite at a time" proposal and how it makes it easy for the client to "give it a try" which gets you in the front door.
9) How to suggest "add-ons" that your client may want and provide extra dollars to your bottom line.

PROPOSAL 3

The Encyclopedia of the Assassination of President John F. Kennedy

Complete Descriptions of Every Person, Place, Object, Event, and Theory Linked to the Assassination of the President

by
James P. Duffy
Vincent L. Ricci

James P. Duffy
Split Rock Farm
RR 1, Box 000
LaGrangeville, NY 00000
(914) 555-1111

This proposal sold for an above-average advance to Thunder's Mouth Press. It was published in the fall of 1992 with the title *The Assassination of John F. Kennedy: A Complete Book of Facts.*

This book sold because of the strong writing credentials of the coauthors and the popularity of the subject matter, but they should have used a harder-sell approach. The proposal is exceptionally well written, but stronger statements would have been better. Never waste opportunities for persuasion.

The proposal might have benefited from standard marketing and promotions sections. The subject is academic, but it could be presented in a highly commercialized manner in view of the continuing "Kennedy craze."

1. This no-nonsense title doesn't require much thought about what this book intends to deliver.

2. The front page is busy. It's usually preferable to have a separate table of contents.

3. It's not necessary to put your address and phone number on a proposal if you're represented by an agent. The publisher shouldn't need to contact you directly unless you have a house editor working on your book.

Outline:

The Encyclopedia of the Assassination of President John F. Kennedy
James P. Duffy & Vincent L. Ricci

4. Mention what the proposed book *is* early in the first or second paragraph, before you mention how much competition it has. It might have been more dramatic to start with some inflammatory statement about the Kennedy assassination itself to pique a publisher's interest. Even though this book is an encyclopedia, it will be read much like a great mystery. This expands its marketing possibilities.

5. The authors handled the issue of competition very cleverly. It's used only as a reason why the proposed book will succeed.

6. This paragraph is a very clear and concise statement of what the book is about. It describes and also persuades.

7. The author should recast this paragraph-long sentence into active voice, rather than passive, as it is now (for example, "The book will embody . . ."). Active voice always appears more confident.

8. This paragraph clearly explains what will be in the book and why it will be unique.

The 20th century has been without question the most turbulent **4** period in world history, embracing two global conflicts, a host of lesser parochial wars, and a fifty-year confrontation of intrigue and military menace between two ideologies championed by opposing superpowers, each possessing the nuclear capability to destroy the planet.

It is a tribute to the charismatic personality of the man, that amid all this turmoil no single event has captured their imagination or fascinated Americans more than the assassination of President John Fitzgerald Kennedy. In the thirty years since his death, reports, accounts, and theories about the popular young president's murder have spawned a steady succession of books, including almost one best- **5** seller a year. The reading public continues to nurture an insatiable curiosity about even the most minute detail concerning the event.

1993 is the 30th anniversary of the assassination and promises to be a stellar year for books, movies, and television specials. Even the world-famous filmmaker Oliver Stone is hard at work on what he promises will be a "big" movie titled *JFK.*

The Encyclopedia of the Assassination of President John F. Kennedy is the **6** ultimate reference for the millions of readers who continue to be fascinated by the Kennedy assassination and the investigations, theories, and controversies surrounding it. A uniquely conceived document, the book is a bulging data bank containing detailed descriptions of every person, place, object, event, and theory connected in any way with the president's death. Each entry has been researched meticulously and clearly reported to produce an original new resource.

An analysis of every theory ever propounded regarding the assas- **7** sination, a complete examination of every piece of evidence known or thought to exist, a full explanation of all facets of conflicting testimony, a discussion and thumbnail sketch of every person involved in any aspect of the assassination or events relating to the crime, and reviews of all books and major articles written about the assassination, investigations, or controversies are all embodied in this work.

No book published since President Kennedy's assassination has **8** done what this book does. The encyclopedic format makes it an easy-to-use reference. One may select a specific subject for review, or simply start at the beginning and read through the entire assassination and the alleged conspiracies connected to the affair.

9   *The Encyclopedia of the Assassination of President John F. Kennedy* will be approximately 150,000 words and take one year to complete.

10 # Author Bios:

The Encyclopedia of the Assassination of President John F. Kennedy

JAMES P. DUFFY is the author of the following books:

Hitler Slept Late and Other Blunders That Cost Him the War
(Praeger Publishers, 1991)
A Military Book Club Selection

You Can Go Bankrupt Without Going Broke
(Pharos Books, 1992)
Coauthored with Lawrence R. Reich, Esq.

Learn While You Sleep: A Remarkable New Way to Learn & Remember
(Avon Books, 1991)

Cutting College Costs
(Harper & Row Publishers, 1988)

How to Earn an Advanced Degree without Going to Graduate School
(Stein & Day/Publishers, 1985)

How to Earn a College Degree without Going to College
(Stein & Day/Publishers, 1983)

Family First Aid Guide
(Harris Publication, 1979)

James P. Duffy and Vincent L. Ricci are coauthors of the following books:

Target Hitler: The Plots to Kill Adolf Hitler
(Praeger Publishers, 1992)
A Military Book Club Main Selection

Czars: The Men and Women Who Ruled Russia for a Thousand Years
(Facts on File, 1993)

Smart Schooling for Smart Kids
(Career Press, 1992)

The Encyclopedia of the Assassination of President John F. Kennedy

A Note to the Reader

When a person, place, etc., is underlined in the text, this indicates that reference has its own listing in the encyclopedia.

9. Assuming the editor has any interest in the book, a preliminary question will be "How long will the book be and when will you finish it?" Your agent can negotiate this for you.

10. The authors aren't celebrities, nor are their professional lives in any way relevant to the subject, so it was fine to avoid extraneous background information and simply state their sizeable and impressive book-writing histories. Although more biographical information would give the team more dimension, their credits show that they will be able to provide a manuscript in a timely and professional manner.

A

11. The sample entries are well written and appear to be well researched. The authors demonstrate that a multitude of obscure and arcane facts and people will be covered extensively.

Strong sample material is often, if not always, the most valuable part of a proposal, since the author needs to answer the most important question of all: What can and will this writer actually do with this concept?

ABADIE, WILLIAM

11

A one-time employee of <u>Jack Ruby,</u> the man who shot and killed <u>Lee Harvey Oswald</u>, Abadie repaired jukeboxes and slot machines for Ruby's gambling operations, and doubled as a bookmaker in one of Ruby's clubs. On December 6, 1963, William Abadie told agents from the <u>Federal Bureau of Investigation</u> that Ruby was well connected with local racketeers and corrupt police officials in both Dallas and Fort Worth, Texas. He also claimed to have seen local police officers hanging out in one of Ruby's bars while illegal gambling activities were in full swing and full sight of the officers.

ABT, JOHN

An attorney with offices in New York City, Abt was noted for his defense of Smith Act violators in 1949. Following his arrest <u>Lee Harvey Oswald</u> attempted to contact Mr. Abt, but was unsuccessful in doing so because the attorney was away from his home on the weekend following the assassination.

PROPOSAL 4

99 Ways to Get the Paperwork Off Your Desk

Double Your Productivity and Eliminate the Drudgework

by Dianna Booher

General Nonfiction — 50,000 words

This book was sold to Warner Books. It was published in 1992 in a quality paperback format with the title *Clean Up Your Act! Effective Ways to Organize Paperwork—And Get It Out of Your Life.* We liked the title used in the proposal because it was easy to visualize and retain. It was not necessary to spend any time telling editors what this book would be about; the title immediately told them what the book offered.

1. The enormity of the paperwork problem is well presented. More importantly, the author shows how the problem deeply affects millions of individual workers, not just the entities for whom they work, thereby suggesting a large consumer market for this information.

Unfamiliar terms such as "knowledge workers" should always be defined on the first reference. Don't shut out your editors with industry terms they may not understand.

Most people consider paperwork the "drudge" part of their jobs. Is there any wonder we have such job turnover and try seven new careers during our lifetime? Much of that shuffling is an attempt to find satisfaction in tasks requiring little or no paperwork—and more time and freedom to "do the real job."

Just how extensive is the paperwork problem? Americans create 30 billion original documents annually. Paperwork costs over $100 billion annually in the U.S. Sixty-five cents of every dollar spent on recordkeeping is wasted on unnecessary files and duplicate information. Seventy-five to 80 percent of documents that we retain we never again refer to.

Today's knowledge workers report that they spend almost half their working day shuffling paper (Source: Our company's survey of 14 companies in seven industries):

Senior executives—46%
Middle managers—45%
Professionals—40%
Clerical support staff—51%

99 Ways to Get the Paperwork Off Your Desk: Double Your Productivity and Eliminate the Drudgework will present tips that "knowledge workers" can use to dig their way out from under the paper blizzard that—

2. An organized list is especially sensible for a book on this subject. The last thing overpapered people need is more paper. They want the remedy to be easily accessible.

- stifles their creativity
- devours their budget and time
- reduces their productivity
- demoralizes their spirit
- angers their customers and colleagues

Popular, New Quick-Reading Format

This book will contain brief entries/tips rather than lengthy chapters. The reader can skim quickly for usable ideas, reading as little or as much explanation as necessary to make personal application of the idea.

3. This is a strong marketing section because all the ideas are fresh and relevant, and it reinforces the book's benefits for the market.

The Market

The book will be aimed at those tired of pushing paper at home and at the office. It would be of particular interest to those one out of our four U.S. workers with a home office and the usual space and support-

³ staff limitations so related to personal productivity and the bottom-line profits in small businesses. Sales reps and PR specialists would have a primary interest because their increased productivity is directly reflected on their commission checks.

Those industrious stay-at-home wives could also pick up tips to improve management of family business and files.

A managerial reader could also apply the tips to his or her department or organization as a whole to improve the communication flow up and down the corporate ladder and eliminate excessive paperwork costs.

Corporations and organizations who sponsor for their employees training courses on management skills, writing, and time-management could certainly use the book as a workshop text.

⁴ # Promotional Ideas

Workshop and Speech Audiences

As a communication consultant to corporate clients and president of my own firm, I and my staff travel nationally and internationally to present these ideas to corporate clients such as IBM, Exxon, and Mobil Oil, among others. All of these audiences are primary buyers of my books. On most occasions, the corporate client buys copies of the book for all meeting attendees. On other occasions where the client organization does not provide books for its employees, we make the books available for back-of-the-room sales and through mail-order.

For example, I recently spoke on this topic at the national convention of the International Association of Convention and Visitor Bureaus, which includes members from all 50 states and 33 foreign countries. Such organizations are potential buyers for further programs and books.

⁵ ## Our Company Mailings

My company does periodic mailings on our books and videos and has an 800 number to take orders generated by radio and TV appearances.

In-House Mailing Lists and Newsletter

We also have an in-house mailing list of INFO TK qualified buyers. In 1992, we started a quarterly newsletter of communication tips, going to attendees of all our past speeches, seminars, and workshops. This newsletter carries ads on our books.

Sidebar notes:

Some marketing sections simply list who the authors think will buy the book, without using the opportunity to persuade.

4. The author provides a menu of ways the book can and will be sold, and supports these with what she has done in the past. The promotional ideas are exceptional. It may be wise to spend some time developing the avenues and resources for promotions. Increasingly, publishers are giving nonfiction acquisition priority to authors who will provide not only the books, but also the means with which to substantially market and promote them. Remember, everything you can do to ensure the success of your book will help tremendously.

5. This author demonstrates access to her market and her viability as a partner in promoting her book. Even if your promotions credentials aren't extensive, any speaking or workshop experience will help. The section is well organized and professional.

Book Packaged with Spin-Off Products Already Produced and Distributed by Nightingale-Conant and Britannica

Nightingale-Conant has produced an audio series based on my communication principles, of which one tape presents some of these paperwork-reduction ideas. Britannica has also produced for corporate trainers two video series based on a few of these selected tips. Both of these companies would be possible distributors, even packaging the book with their audio and video series. Britannica currently distributes many of my other books to corporate buyers.

6. This is a novel, well-thought-out idea. It takes more than talent to be a successful nonfiction writer. It helps to understand something about business and creative marketing.

Contest for Digging Out from Under the Paper Blizzard   6

A possible "gimmick" to generate media interest in the book could include small prizes (such as dictating equipment, computers, new decorator file cabinets, or electronic mail systems) for readers who make the most improvements in reduced paperwork. Individuals who rid themselves of paper clutter could document such change by submitting "before" and "after" photos of their desks or offices. We could select the four or five individuals who make the most drastic improvement, and ask manufacturers to donate the products as prizes in exchange for the media coverage.

7. It's interesting that the author is essentially competing with herself. She confronts this fact and strengthens her case. It would have been foolish to ignore the fact that several good time-management/organization books exist, and the author doesn't try. Instead, she uses their abundance as a selling point—after all, these books got published and succeeded for a reason. She also explains how her book will cut a relatively unique niche.

The Competition   7

No other book on the market deals with this subject specifically.

My previous book *Cutting Paperwork in the Corporate Culture* (Facts on File, 1986) deals with a similar issue—reducing paperwork in the large corporation. This book received wide media coverage and was named to Executive Soundview Summaries' list of "25 Best Business Books of the 1980s." (See attached listing.)

The proposed book will differ from this one in that the new book will focus on help for the *individual* rather than paperwork systems and management in the large organization. The tips will focus on ways to increase *personal* productivity for those who don't have the clout to change things throughout his or her organization.

Many of the tips can be applied at home as well as at work.

Not just another how-to-organize-the-family-records book: On a similar topic, *Taming the Paper Tiger: Organizing the Paper in Your Life* (by Barbara Hemphill; Dodd, Mead, 1988) focuses on the *family* paperwork pile at home rather than at work. That book gives direction only with what to discard, what to file, and how to file it.

7 *Not just another time-management/organization book:* The many successful books on time-management and personal organization deal with organizing your time, space, and life. But they do not have the specific focus of paperwork. For example, instead of telling a reader how to use time efficiently to write a report (i.e., concentrate, use peak-energy periods, delegate), this new book will tell the reader which kinds of reports and memos to eliminate altogether!

Evidence of the still unaddressed paperwork problem: The extreme popularity and excellent sales records of books written on the time-management facet of the paperwork problem evidence the need for such a book:

> *Getting Organized* (Stephanie Winston, Norton, 1978; Warner 1981)
> *The Organized Executive* (Stephanie Winston, Warner, 1985)
> *Time for Success* (Alec MacKenzie, McGraw-Hill, 1989)
> *Doing It Now* (Edwin Bliss, Bantam, 1984)
> *Getting Things Done* (Edwin Bliss, Bantam, 1978)
> *If You Haven't Got the Time to Do It Right, When Will You Find the Time to Do It Over?* (Jeffrey J. Mayer, Simon and Schuster, 1990)
> *The Ninety-Minute Hour* (Jay Levinson, Dutton, 1990)

The proposed book should meet with similar success to these time-management best-sellers because it will address the same needs. But it should be even more helpful to the individual because it will go further with specific how-to's of paperwork—the biggest timewaster of all.

8 # About the Author

Dianna Booher, a business-communication consultant, is the founder and president of Booher Writing Consultants, with offices in Houston and Dallas. She and her staff travel nationally and internationally speaking and presenting communication workshops to governmental agencies and corporate clients. Her clients include IBM, Exxon, Mobil Oil, Shell Oil, Hewlett-Packard, ENRON, Unisys, MidCon United, Pennzoil, Conoco, Tenneco, Texas Instruments, Coopers & Lybrand, Marriott Corporation, USA Today, Department of the Army, the Federal Aviation Administration, National Telephone Cooperatives Association, National Rural Electric Association, among others.

Her audiences include employees of varying work experience— from senior executives to middle managers, entry-level professionals,

8. As with most of the authors who generously allowed their proposals to be showcased here, this author has excellent credentials and knows how to say it without sounding conceited. She included fine state-of-the-art promotional brochures as part of the package.

Don't let these sample bio sections intimidate you or—even worse—discourage you from participating in the process. A good idea, if handled correctly, can overcome most weaknesses you may have in the bio department.

and clerical support staff. Additionally, she speaks at national conven- 8
tions to groups as diverse as corporate training directors (American
Society for Training and Development) and agricultural researchers
and administrators (the American Farm Bureau Federation).

Besides consulting, public speaking, and seminar presentations,
Dianna has published 24 books, 13 in the area of communications.
Several of these books have been selected by book clubs for their prac-
tical advice to the general reader: Book-of-the-Month/Fortune Book
Club, Macmillan Executive Program, Writer's Digest Book Club,
American Management Association Book Club, and McGraw-Hill
Book Club.

The books have also gained positive media attention in publica-
tions as diverse as *USA Today*, *Sylvia Porter's Personal Finance Magazine*,
The New Woman, *Working Woman*, *National Enquirer*, *The Detroit News*,
the *Los Angeles Times*, the *Houston Chronicle*, *The Dallas Morning News*,
Management Development Report, *Research Institute of America*, *Industry
Week*, *Executive Excellence*, *Training and Development Journal*, *Personnel
Journal*, *Glamour*, and *Seventeen*, among numerous other professional
journals and general-interest publications.

In conjunction with Britannica Educational Corporation, Dianna
has produced a videotape series of her writing program, *Basic Steps for
Better Business Writing*, and two video programs, *Cutting Paperwork in the
Corporate Culture: Management Strategies* and *Cutting Paperwork in the
Corporate Culture: Support Staff Strategies*. Her business writing principles
also are the subject of *Business Writing: Quick, Clear, Concise*, a video produced by American Media. Nightingale-Conant has produced two
audio series based on her corporate communication expertise entitled
Write to the Point: Business Communications from Memos to Meetings and
How to Be an Effective Executive Assistant. Victor Books has also released
her audio program, *The Confident Communicator*.

Ms. Booher holds a master's degree in English, with a specialization in writing, from the University of Houston.

9. This is a good way to list the author's many publications.

Publications by Dianna Booher   9

Books
The Complete Letterwriter's Almanac (Prentice-Hall, October 1991)

Executive's Portfolio of Model Speeches (Prentice-Hall, July 1991)

The Confident Communicator (Victor Books, October 1990)

Writing for Technical Professionals (John Wiley & Sons, Spring 1989)

[9] *To the Letter: A Handbook of Model Letters for the Busy Executive* (Lexington Books, February 1988)

Good Grief, Good Grammar: A Businessperson's Guide to Grammar and Usage (Facts on File, February 1988; Fawcett, 1989; Writer's Digest Book Club)

First Thing Monday Morning (Fleming H. Revell, 1988)

Cutting Paperwork in the Corporate Culture (Facts on File, September 1986; Macmillan Executive Book Club; Book-of-the-Month/Fortune Book Club; Newstrack Executive Summaries)

The New Secretary: How to Handle People As Well As You Handle Paper (Facts on File, 1985)

Send Me a Memo (Facts on File, 1984; Macmillan Executive Program; American Management Association Book Club; Book-of-the-Month/Fortune Book Club; and McGraw-Hill Book Club)

Would You Put That in Writing? (Facts on File, 1983; HarperCollins, 1985, paper; Macmillan Executive Program; *Library Journal*'s selection of best business books of 1983)

Boy Friends and Boyfriends (Fleming H. Revell, Spring 1988)

They're Playing Our Secret (Fleming H. Revell, Spring 1988)

That Book's Not in Our Library (Fleming H. Revell, Spring 1988)

Love, Love (Messner/Simon and Schuster, 1985)

Getting Along with People Who Don't Get Along (Broadman, 1984; Broadman Book Club)

Making Friends with Yourself and Other Strangers (Messner/Simon and Schuster, 1982)

Rape: What Would You Do If. . .? (Messner/Simon and Schuster, 1981; paper, 1983; American Library Association's Best Books for Young Adults, 1981)

Not Yet Free (Broadman, 1981)

The Last Caress (Zebra, 1981)

The Faces of Death (Broadman, 1980)

Coping When Your Family Falls Apart (Messner/Simon and Schuster, 1979)

Help, We're Moving! (Messner/Simon and Schuster, 1984; Broadman, paper, 1978)

Audio Series

People Power: Tips for Successful Secretaries, Executive and Administrative Assistants, or Office Managers (Booher Consultants, April 1992)

Get Your Book Publi$hed! (Booher Consultants, October 1991)

Write to the Point: Business Communications from Memos to Meetings (Nightingale-Conant, January 1990)

The Confident Communicator (VistaMedia, October 1990)

Videotape Series

Business Writing: Quick, Clear, Concise (American Media, 1992)

Basic Steps for Better Business Writing (Britannica Business and Industry Films, 1985)

Cutting Paperwork in the Corporate Culture: Management Strategies (Encyclopaedia Britannica, 1989)

Cutting Paperwork in the Corporate Culture: Support Staff Strategies (Encyclopaedia Britannica, 1989)

Computer Software Package

Sharpening Your Executive Writing (KJ Software, 1985)

Musical Dramas

For Me, It Was Different (The Benson Company, 1984)

Christmases of Your Life (The Benson Company, 1983)

10. This book is unusual in that each chapter is essentially a brief, single idea (what the electronic media refer to as a "soundbite"). Each chapter can be understood adequately by its title alone, so chapter abstracts would be superfluous. The only weakness in this outline is that the author doesn't really explain how the chapters will become a book. It would help to have some explanation of format so the publisher knows how the list is to be expanded and integrated.

Table of Contents

Part 1: Handling Your Outgoing Responses

11. Highlight/personalize brochures for customers; avoid the form cover letter response to inquiries.
12. Stay in touch with friends, colleagues, and clients in useful ways rather than formal business letters (clipped articles with handwritten note, and so forth).
13. Use margin notes for replies.
14. Use "stamped" replies.
15. Pay bills only twice a month; file receipts immediately.
16. Dictate.
17. Compose your own documents on the word processor.
18. Eliminate meaningless confirmations of phone conversations.
19. Eliminate most cover letters.
20. Squelch the urge to confirm everything in writing.
21. Eliminate most trip reports.
22. Eliminate computer printouts of uninterpretable information.
23. Eliminate weekly/monthly activity reports.
24. Eliminate duplicate information submitted in multiple formats.
25. Eliminate minutes for most meetings.
26. Ask why when *anyone* asks for a report, and suggest alternatives.
27. Use "exception" reporting to your boss.
28. Use idea wheels for to-do lists.
29. Use idea wheels for project planning.
30. Use idea wheels for problem-analysis and decision-making.
31. Use idea wheels for meeting agendas and assignments.
32. Use idea wheels to record client conversations.
33. Substitute dynamic visuals for lengthy reports.
34. Use electronic message systems.
35. Find out what goes where and why. Stop sending the unnecessary.
36. Reconsider the idea, "I can do it better/faster myself."
37. Delegate effectively—with full authority and clear instructions.
38. Work ahead of deadlines.
39. Use deadlines to your benefit and to motivate yourself to better work.
40. Create a climate of trust to eliminate self-protective writing.
41. Consider the cost and time in double-checking.
42. Aim to do it right the first time.
43. Develop a personal style/writing guide for recurring questions.
44. Use the MADE format for delivering all phone, in-person, and written messages.
45. Learn which details to include in your formal correspondence and reports.
46. "Layer" your documents for the appropriate audiences.

47. Be direct when you write—use specific, clear words and simple sentences.
48. Judge length by reading time and access, not paper or pages.
49. Forget the idea that "more is better."
50. Practice completed staff work.
51. Determine a hierarchy of values for editing and rewriting.
52. Stifle the urge to edit others' writing for editing's sake.
53. Update your distribution lists and consider the "need to know."
54. Stop sending things until people ask for them.
55. Help people route what you write.
56. Post information of general interest.
57. Write and post instructions to operate equipment.
58. Write and duplicate fliers containing answers to frequently asked questions.
59. Develop personalized models of letters and memos frequently sent.
60. Use form letters/memos for internal audiences.
61. Use personal, applicable letters/memos to customers.
62. Talk rather than write to give mild reprimands.
63. Talk rather than write to send trial balloons.
64. Talk rather than write to persuade the uninterested.
65. Talk rather than write to negotiate small details.
66. Talk rather than write to get immediate feedback.
67. Talk rather than write when you need to see a reaction to your message.
68. Talk rather than write when "how you say it" is as important as "what you say."
69. Use an assistant to pre-write.
70. Use an assistant to pre-read.
71. Ask what goes where and why; eliminate redundancy.
72. Establish priorities.
73. Psyche yourself out of procrastination.
74. Use prime time on pay-off paper.
75. Do the necessary paperwork when nobody else is—in odd times without interruptions or in the most uninterrupted place and time possible.
76. Keep others informed so they can shoulder the load.
77. Do your work by phone when you're out of the office; don't play paperwork pile-up while you're away.
78. Listen to/read instructions, and do it right the first time.

Part 2: Handling Incoming Information

79. Ignore responses that can be directed elsewhere.
80. Put destruction dates on paper.
81. Purge your files every time you open them.
82. Cross-reference papers rather than make/store extra copies.
83. Put paperwork aside only if you've made a complete notation about what needs to be done or how it will be used later.
84. File research by use or event, not by subject.
85. Request and keep multiple copies of "permanent" records/ certificates.
86. File warranties and instructions logically and permanently, with receipts.
87. Treat family/home files as seriously as you do business files.
88. Get off others' distribution lists.
89. Use electronic message systems.
90. Give recognition to achievements not recorded on paper.
91. Take talk seriously.
92. Reward ideas to cut paperwork.
93. Don't behead the bearer of bad news.
94. Let others know they can be straightforward with you.
95. Understand the real cost of processing forms.
96. Use well-designed forms.
97. Use a clipping service for subjects of interest.
98. Don't let your computer reproduce endlessly and aimlessly.
99. Discard unread magazines, journals, and newspapers.

" Sample Entries

Tip No. 2   Read faster and with purpose.

Let's face it: When the mail advertising comes in, we can go through it in 30 seconds, dumping most. Or we can spend half an hour reading every word. But we shouldn't let those who mail to us impose on our time any more than we let those who phone us.

Now, before all of you who use direct mail in your marketing efforts tune out, let me elaborate. I didn't say to ignore your mail. Just be choosy. What many consider "junk" mail may be valuable to you personally. From your daily mail, you may glean new product or service ideas, marketing ideas, interesting statistics, solutions to your problems, or amusing anecdotes. One person's junk mail is another's treasure. But we need to be selective.

11. We've included one of the several sample chapters the author provided. The samples were important because they showed the editors what the book would look like. At a few hundred words per chapter, writing them was not an excessive effort.

For those things you really want to read—and I subscribe to 19 such publications—schedule uninterrupted reading time and get your money's worth. But for the so-so publications, the mail, the memos, and the reports that need responses from you, have an assistant pre-read and call your attention to things that need action. In fact, even in reading professional journals, an assistant can highlight key ideas that will be of particular interest.

Reading everything put before you should not be a compulsive habit. Read only what you really want and need to read.

PROPOSAL 5

Run Through Walls!

Breaking Down Barriers with Creative Sales Techniques and Tips from the Superstars

by
Barry J. Farber
and
Joyce Wycoff

Business/Sales—50,000 words

Copyright 1990 by Barry Farber and Joyce Wycoff

This proposal was acquired by Prentice Hall and published with the title *Breakthrough Selling: Customer-Building Strategies from the Best in the Business*. The book was a main selection of the Fortune Book Club and was also highly recommended by *Success* magazine.

The authors were strongly attached to the proposed title, but the publisher changed it in part because a marketing book had recently been published with the same title. Book titles can usually be legally duplicated, but to avoid confusion, publishers tend to not repeat existing titles.

It's a strong proposal, but it was relatively difficult to sell because there's so much competition in this area.

However, this proposal has so many exceptional aspects to it that it sold anyway. You should read it several times for the full effect.

1. The "Brief Description" is interesting, but it could be even stronger. The authors begin with a strong lead, but dilute it with an immediate synopsis of someone else's book. They could have brought in the concept of a return to basics by a direct focus on *Run Through Walls!*

2. It also would have helped if the authors had visually separated the four elements of the "bag of tricks" with subheads or a bulleted list.

Brief Description

In the past several years, corporate America began to recognize that something was wrong. Decades devoted to short-term earnings and the technicalities of management and financial analysis weren't working. Industry after industry was rocked by foreign competition. "Made in Japan" became a sign of excellence and "service" became a scarcity.

Peters and Waterman wrote a watershed book that called for a return to basics—service, quality and a focus on people. Their "search for excellence" found that a commitment to these basics also resulted in a better bottom line.

The authors of *Run Through Walls!* talked to hundred of salespeople, sales managers, sales trainers and top management to find the common trends among the top sales performers. The result was an overriding commitment to the basics—again, service, quality and a focus on people. The sales stars did not depend on fancy closing techniques, tricks or gimmicks. They did not rely on manipulation or psychology. Their "bag of tricks" held an uncommon ability to build relationships, an overwhelming belief in the excellence of their product and company, a commitment to providing the best service possible, and an ability to identify and find solutions for customer problems.

Run Through Walls! outlines series of powerful tools that have helped thousands of salespeople improve their skills and reinforces those tools with interviews from some of the most masterful salespeople in America. The interviews give several different slants on the tools and how they can be used in any area of sales. The sales stars interviewed are from different industries and from large companies and small. They include masters who have been in sales for years and rookies who have identified key skills early in their careers.

3. What is a "mindmap"? Always define unclear terms the first time they're used if they wouldn't be readily understood otherwise.

4. In a book of this kind, its thesis or program aspect should be laid out as clearly as possible. The only real weakness in this proposal is that the book itself isn't immediately apparent from the description.

Each chapter includes an action plan to help the reader incorporate the tools and tips into his sales and success program. Chapters are concluded with a mindmap to reinforce the chapter material and to help the reader assimilate the powerful tool of mindmapping.

The authors are committed to making *Run Through Walls!* a best-seller and have developed a unique marketing plan to work in concert with the publisher's marketing efforts. Provided here are an overview of the marketing plan and a synopsis of the book based on the first half of the interviews. We will incorporate new material, tools and stories as they are gathered from the remaining interviews and from discussions with salespeople, trainers and management.

Market

5 Sales is the last profession where the American Dream still prevails. The Bureau of Labor Statistics estimates a total sales force of over 13 million nationally. Lured by "no-limit" incomes, self-determined hours, the glamour of travel and endless company-paid lunches, many of these would-be sales-people are mashed down, chewed up and spit out long before their commissions cover even the minimum wage.

5. It's always good to document your target market(s) with proven numbers.

But the lure remains. Some experts estimate that as many as 100,000 new salespeople enter the labor force each year—replacing others who have been promoted or redirected to other pastures. Like most frontiers, sales is beginning to be tamed and civilized. Although the fringes will always be wild and wooly with bright-eyed youngsters and calloused old-timers, the main-stream of sales is passing into a real profession demanding dedication, education, integrity and abundant amounts of perseverance.

6 In no other field is the relationship between personal effort and personal reward so direct. As the demand for sophistication increases, salespeople are continuously looking for new information and techniques to help them improve their skills and build sales. *Personal Selling Power*'s readers survey shows that salespeople purchase a median of 6 books per year primarily in the areas of selling techniques and success motivation. It seems salespeople will invest in any book or material which will help them improve their success rate.

6. These paragraphs build a case for the market potential. They are persuasive and also reinforce the concepts of the book. Citing the six books purchased per salesperson is an effective statistic.

The market for sales reference material continuously renews itself as large numbers of salespeople drop out or burn out. The market for these is growing even more as leaders in business and industry recognize that all employees are part of the sales force. Bill Razzouk, Vice President of U.S. Sales for Federal Express, was recently asked how many salespeople were employed by Federal Express. His reply was: "Every employee sells."

Run Through Walls! is about techniques which will help every salesperson increase sales. It is also about building relationships with customers—getting to know customers and their needs, learning to identify problems they may not even know exist and then solving them. *Run Through Walls!* demonstrates how to develop a service philosophy that creates long-term, repeat customers. The techniques and philosophies in this book can be adapted to every area of business.

7 *Run Through Walls!* may not appeal to everybody. Many business people have not understood that selling is basic to their business success, and many salespeople believe they know all there is to know. It *will* appeal to salespeo-

7. This paragraph is very clever.

ple and business people who are constantly looking for new techniques and tips to improve their skills. It will appeal to trainers and managers who are looking for new materials to help their sales force.

The best-selling business books of the past decade have had some common traits. Books such as *In Search of Excellence, The One Minute Manager* and *Swim with the Sharks* have all had a title which was intriguing and appealing; a fast, easily read style; an abundance of examples and stories (except for *The One Minute Manager* which is a story), and a message which is as powerful as it is basic. *Run Through Walls!* shares those traits. The title, message and look of the book will convey the message that this is a practical, easily accessible book to help the reader become more successful in whatever endeavor he attempts. For example:

Title: The title has received overwhelming approval by everyone who has been exposed to it. It is active, visual and quickly tells the reader that here is something that is going to help him break through barriers. The title is based on a quote by Jan Carlzon, CEO of Scandinavian Airlines, acknowledged as one of the best airline companies in the world. (We hope to get Carlzon to write the introduction to the book.)

Readability: Readers today want to get a practical message quickly. *Run Through Walls!* will be quick and fun to read. The book should have a layout which invites people to browse—such as *Information Anxiety*—with set-outs, boxes, illustrations, cartoons and other visuals to help the reader get the message quickly. We have a cartoonist working on illustrations for key points.

Interviews: Probably the most catching feature of the book is the interviews with the top sales stars. Here in one place, the reader will find the industry leaders giving advice on how to be more successful. Stories from the sales stars are often funny, always motivational. These stories and examples from many different industries will help the reader understand how to implement the tools, tips and techniques in his own situations.

Competition

8. The competition section accurately and wisely acknowledges the many sales books in print. Never try to conceal the obvious. The authors adequately express why their work will distinguish itself in a glutted market. They should also have reiterated that the large number of sales books in print reflects a hungry and self-renewing market that buys an above-average number of books.

There are a lot of sales books on the market. Some do extremely well such as Tom Hopkins' *How to Master the Art of Selling* and Joe Girard's books. Many sell only a moderate number of copies. After talking to salespeople, sales

8 trainers, sales managers, and senior managers, we identified some common problems with most of the books on the market.

Too theoretical—many sales book authors are academics or consultants who take a very theoretical approach to sales. There is an abundance of sales "models" and technical approaches to closing, prospecting, and negotiating. Salespeople want practical tips which can be put to use immediately.

Too difficult to read—time is a precious commodity to salespeople. They want to be able to quickly get the message and find the tips and techniques that will help build sales.

Single Focus—most sales books are written from the perspective of a single industry and a single salesperson. All sales situations are different and salespeople need a lot of ideas and examples so they can pick the ones that fit their situations.

Run Through Walls! is a sales book that is easy and fun to read, contains tips and techniques that can be immediately implemented and gives comments and examples from top salespeople in many different industries and geographical locations. During the process of interviewing for the book, we asked each of the salespeople, sales managers, sales trainers and managers what they would look for in a book they would recommend to their staff. *Run Through Walls!* was designed to meet their needs and incorporates their ideas and suggestions.

Marketing Plan

9 Harvey Mackay has recently proved that marketing can take an "ok" book and make it a phenomenon. We are applying Mackay's principles of marketing to *Run Through Walls!* and building a marketing plan that will guarantee a best-seller. Both of the coauthors are committed to doing everything necessary to make *Run Through Walls!* the next business blockbuster. The basics of this plan are as follows:

Endorsements:

10 We anticipate having approximately 50 top salespeople, sales trainers and sales managers interviewed in the book. Most of the people interviewed to

9. This is a pretty big promise. Let's see how the authors plan to deliver on it.

10. Note some of these great marketing ideas. Even if you don't put them into your proposal, keep them in mind for after your book is published. The great selling point in this case is that the marketing plan is reasonable and shows a strong profit potential for the publisher. If you can show that you'll contribute greatly to the book's success, it will enhance your chances for a sale. Don't make claims you can't fulfill, though—word travels fast.

date expressed an active interest in having the book available for their sales 10 staff. Some comments received are:

> "If *Run Through Walls!* is as powerful as I believe it will be, I will provide it to all my staff. I will also recommend to Ricoh that they make it available to all Ricoh dealers and sales representatives through a co-op program." Art Mahony, Regional Marketing Manager, Ricoh

> "A book like *Run Through Walls!* that will give me insight on successful solution selling would be highly recommended to my staff. I would also send the book to the head of sales training for distribution to our sales force." Bill Stack, Manager, Eastern Communications Region, GE Information Services

> "If *Run Through Walls!* has information that my sales staff can apply immediately, I would go out and buy it for distribution at our sales meetings." Betsy Martin, Advertising Sales Director, *Money* Magazine

11. These appear to be trustworthy promises—but, of course, they're nonbinding. Publishers (and agents) are skeptical about nonbinding promises.

> "If a book was made with examples of success stories from top sales-11 people and how they became successful, I would have all my salespeople in the Electrolux organization buy it." Rich Luisi, Regional Manager, Electrolux

> "Any book that has successful ideas and stories from top salespeople would be read by all my salespeople." Steve Dantus, Senior Managing Director, Bear Stearns

Interviews have been scheduled with the following companies but do not appear in the synopsis:

Apple Computer
Armstrong World Industries
Prudential Insurance
Xerox
IBM
Joe Paterno
Coca Cola
Sara Lee
Johnson & Johnson
Personal Selling Power
Chrysler
Franklin International Institute

In addition to the people interviewed in the book, we expect to have endorsements from:

12

> Tom Peters, consultant & author
> Harvey Mackay, CEO Mackay Envelopes
> Al Ries, author Marketing Warfare
> Charles Garfield, author Peak Performance
> Jan Carlzon, CEO Scandinavian Airlines
> Barney Sofro, CEO House of Fabrics
> Fred Smith, CEO Federal Express
> Denis Waitley, speaker & author
> Ken Blanchard, speaker & author

12. Impressive endorsements by themselves won't create a best-seller, but they can be an important element in the decision to publish your book.

We would also expect to get many more endorsements after we have the manuscript finished. People are so busy today that they cannot afford to spend time on a book that isn't going to be worth their while—therefore, the endorsements are a critical part of the book marketing. We will spend a great deal of effort making sure that we have endorsements from all types of people and from all different industries and types of organizations.

Magazine Articles

The authors have been published by several of the major magazines and have developed a working relationship with many editors. We have talked to them about this book project and they are very interested in publishing articles from the book. Because of the nature of the book with its personalities and stories, it will be possible to develop several unique focuses for the different publications.

13   Here is a listing of the magazines and editors that have been developed to date:

Sales & Marketing Management Magazine
    Contact: Martin Everett—General Editor
                     Arthur Bragg—Senior Editor
                     Bill Keenan—Managing Editor
    Article: "Have Your Customer Run Your Next Meeting" (April, 1990 issue, feature article)

Training Magazine
    Contact: Jack Gordon—Editor
                     Bob Filipczak—New Products Editor
    Article: "Achieving Quota Through Your Reps NOT for Your Reps" (March, 1990 issue)

13. This section is unclear. It could be a strong selling point, but there are too many unanswered questions. These were potential media placements, but it's not immediately apparent from how the information is presented. It would be better to explain that the article titles are proposed topics for these magazines stemming from the book.

If this point is made clearly, it will show that even though the claims are speculative, the authors are hard workers and are well connected with the relevant media.

Training and Development Journal
> **Contact**:   Patricia Galagan—Editor
>   Liz Olivetti—Editor Assistant
> **Article**:   Submitted for review "How to Measure Sales Training"

Tom Peters On Achieving Excellence
> **Contact**:   Paul M. Cohen—Editor
> **Article**:   "Customer Run Meetings" (May, 1990 issue)

Personal Selling Power
> **Contact**:   Gerhard Gschwandtner—Publisher
>   Jamie Fear—Production Editor
> **Article**:   "Using Tape Recorded Interviews Can Give You A Competitive Gauge" (May/June, 1988 issue)
>   "Increasing Your Sales with Customer Satisfaction Surveys" (Jan/Feb, 1990 issue)

Creative Training Techniques
> **Contact**:   Brian McDermott—Editorial Director
> **Quoted**:   January, 1990 and February, 1990 issues

Success Magazine
> **Contact**:   Don Wallace—Senior Editor
>   Duncan Anderson—Senior Editor
> **Article**:   "Customer Satisfaction Surveys" (May, 1990 issue)

Recognition and Promotions Business
> **Contact**:   Heather Herbertson—Associate Editor
> **Article**:   "Brainstorming: A New Look at an Old Technique" (December/January, 1990 issue)

By the time the book is completed, we intend to have strong contacts and commitments from other major business and general interest publications such as *Inc., Fortune, Entrepreneur,* various in-flight magazines, and as many of the trade publications as possible. We want to have as many articles as possible released around the time of the release of the book and would plan on working with the publisher's marketing department to coordinate the release.

14. The plan for creating marketing representatives is wonderful. If your book lends itself to this kind of follow-up and relationship building—by all means do it.

Marketing Representatives

As we have interviewed salespeople, sales managers, and sales trainers for the book, we have worked to build relationships with each person interviewed. Each of the sales stars interviewed receives a thank you note from Barry and

¹⁴ a thank you letter from Joyce with a package of motivational quote cards. Each star is put on the mailing list to receive *Mindplay* with a "Compliments of Barry Farber and Joyce Wycoff" note attached. Over the next several months that it takes to finish the manuscript and prepare it for release, the interviewees will receive monthly notes and status reports and bits and pieces of information about the book.

Once the book is released, each interviewee will be presented with a special plaque, a special *Run Through Walls!* pin and an autographed copy of the book at a presentation at his/her company. We want each person interviewed to feel that this is their book—that they played a major part in bringing it to being. We believe they will be a major part of the success of the book and will be, in effect, marketing representatives for the book. Since the 50 people we interviewed will be backed by a combined sales staff of approximately 50,000 people, their active involvement can represent a major part of the book launch.

Since the book is applicable for people beyond those strictly classified as salespeople, the sales stars represent a much larger base of interested parties—for example Federal Express alone has almost 90,000 employees and they are all considered salespeople. We intend for the top management of each of the star's companies to receive complimentary, autographed copies of the book.

One indication that we have received already of the interest that the book is generating within an organization is at Northwestern Mutual Life Insurance. Dennis Tamcsin requested additional information about the book (and its possible release date) so that he could talk about it in a speech before 250 of Northwestern's general agents.

¹⁵ Also, Marc Roberts, boxing promoter, has indicated that once the book is available and after a successful championship fight, we will have Ray Mercer (who recently won the IBF championship) hold up the book during an interview and talk about how the book has helped him with motivation and commitment. Mercer was the leadoff boxer in recent mega-event fights—the viewership of the Hearns/Leonard fight was estimated at over 200 million. Roberts is interested in working with us to make this an interesting public relations event.

¹⁶ Publicist

We have arranged for XYZ Public Relations and Associates to handle the publicity for the book. She will be arranging television shows (such as the "Larry King Show," "Good Morning America," etc.), radio talk shows and appearances. Both coauthors expect to devote a minimum of three months in an intense publicity campaign.

15. This is innovative, and it's effective for the authors to be this expansive about their self-marketing agenda. Again, remember that without a binding commitment, such ideas have limited value.

16. Don't be intimidated if you don't have your own publicist, but don't be shy if you do. Media exposure is a plus. If you have contacts, say so.

We think there will be several angles to hang these appearances on—one will be "Corporate America's Unsung Heroes." There is every indication that the top sales stars have known for years that customer orientation was the key to success, that service was the glue that held business together. While the rest of corporate America was going down the MBA/spreadsheet rabbit hole, millions of heroes were going out of their way to give excellent service, to fix problems, to listen to the needs of customers and to develop long-term relationships in a short-term, quarterly-stock-price-mentality world.

We will be working with the PR firm to schedule as many television and [17] radio shows as possible. Whenever possible, we will have the sales stars appear with us on the television shows.

Retailer and Wholesalers

Following the lead of Harvey Mackay, we intend to make presentations to the major book retailers and wholesalers. We will make personal presentations to B. Dalton, Waldenbooks, Crown and Ingram Books to make sure that the advance orders are substantial. A mailing will go out to bookstore retailers announcing the release and building interest in the book. An incentive program will be worked out with the distributors to provide a *Run Through Walls!* pin for each book store that orders over 10 copies of the book.

We will back the book with an unconditional guarantee. If the reader [18] doesn't get at least one idea that will help him *Run Through Walls!* and break through barriers, he can send the book back and we will refund his money.

Seminars and Direct Mail

The authors will be offering the book at training sessions, seminars, lectures, [19] and through a direct mail program. We will also be working with other organizations such as University Associates and Lakewood Publications to have the book offered in their catalogs.

The authors will also be developing a tape series based on *Run Through Walls!* material. This series will complement and reinforce the visibility of the book.

Marketing Summary   [20]

The authors are committed to *Run Through Walls!* We will do everything necessary to make it a top seller. We expect to invest a major portion of our advance in the marketing activities outlined above. We will work with the publisher to insure that our investment and efforts are coordinated with the pub-

---

17. This counts. Hiring your own PR firm (which the authors did) is music to a publisher's ears. We want to stress, however, that these authors had a much broader agenda than simply being authors; they were promoting their respective consulting businesses. If you make such a claim, the publisher may require that it be included in your contract.

18. This gimmick takes a lot of "chutzpah" (guts), but if you can afford it, why not? Be as creative as you can.

19. Authors who frequently speak to large audiences are especially attractive to publishers because of their back-of-the-room sales potential. More details should have been provided about how many appearances are made each year and how many people are reached.

20. Offering to invest in marketing is highly optional for those of you who, like most working

[20] lisher's efforts and will be available for any promotional activities scheduled by the publisher.

Shortly after contract negotiations, we would like to schedule a meeting to develop a coordinated marketing plan with the publisher's staff. We are confident that the message of *Run Through Walls!* is powerful and important. Only by developing an outstanding marketing plan can we insure that this message is delivered to the maximum number of readers.

About the Authors

[21] **Barry J. Farber**, president of Farber Training Systems, Inc., has successfully trained thousands of salespeople, sales managers, and trainers with high-impact, tailor-made workshops. Some of the companies he has trained include: Minolta, Schering-Plough, Ricoh, Club Med, Gestetner, and many others. He is also the president of M.A.P. Systems Inc., a company that distributes time-management and organizational tools.

Prior to founding F.T.S. and M.A.P. Systems, Inc., Barry has been selling since 1975 and has held positions in sales management, sales training, and was the national sales-training manager for a 3.5 billion dollar corporation.

Barry has also been featured on national radio and television shows and written numerous articles for leading sales and management publications, some of which include: *Success* magazine, *Sales and Marketing Management*, *Personal Selling Power*, *Training* magazine, *Reseller Management*, and *Tom Peters—On Achieving Excellence*.

Joyce Wycoff is a corporate consultant, trainer and writer in the areas of innovation, team building and communication. She has a broad background in management and combines a "bottom-line" orientation with possibility thinking to help people up to new innovative ways to solve problems and improve productivity.

Joyce is the editor and publisher of the newsletter *MindPlay* devoted to innovation and creativity in business and she is the author of *Mindmapping: A New Way to Use Your Brain* (published by Berkley Publishing Group, release early 1991) and lives with her husband, Richard, and dog, Rumple, in San Diego.

Barry and Joyce met through *MindPlay* when Barry submitted an article for publication. After many discussions of philosophies and possibilities, they decided to team up and write a book that combined sales and creativity techniques and gave salespeople specific tools to build their sales.

writers, rely on your advance money to eat; but it does convey a prosperous image. These claims are ambitious, sincere, and innovative, but not nearly enough to guarantee the promise that the book would be a best-seller. Nowhere are the authors explicit about dedicating their own money. It was the proposal's editorial merits as well as the authors' genuine credibility and personal commitment that made it possible to close a deal.

21. This is an effective and persuasive "About the Authors" section because the authors not only have strong credentials, but they also use what's relevant to the project's success.

22. The outline should be better organized. The focus of the book seems fuzzy compared to the strong marketing strategy. It might have helped to begin the outline with a more pointedly worded section heading—something like "Breaking Barriers"—to keep in line with the title and style of the book.

Table of Contents

Overview: The Sales Process

23. The title for Chapter 7 seems a bit cryptic without being intriguing. Even if the author intends to clear up the terminology in the chapter summary, it might have been wise to make the title less esoteric in the first place.

Epilogue **Putting It All Together: The Book**
Using all the tools and techniques to create a best-seller

Synopsis

Overview: The Sales Process

24 In a quieter, simpler time a manufacturer could build a better mousetrap and the world would beat a path to his door. Today there is no path and the world doesn't even know about the mousetrap . . . and may not even know the manufacturer. The key to bringing the world and the mousetrap together is the salesperson. The salesperson is the catalyst in the sales process—the active ingredient that combines the customer's wants or needs and the product's benefit to satisfy a need or solve a problem.

To play this role the salesperson needs to have a certain set of information and skills including:

- an in-depth knowledge of the product or service
- comprehensive understanding of the customer's needs
- the creativity to make connections
- the ability to establish a strong, trusting relationship with the customer

Each of us is a salesperson—we sell our ideas, we sell ourselves, we sell our time. Every business transaction is made between someone who wants to sell something and someone who wants to have the benefit of the product, service or idea being sold.

Accountants sell management on the accuracy and importance of financial reports, engineers sell ideas for new products, and lawyers sell security and peace of mind. Our politicians, parents, teachers, and preachers all sell us their values and visions of a better world. If we didn't want what they were selling, we wouldn't buy it . . . and they would no longer be in business.

Our ability to succeed in life depends to a great extent on how well we understand the process of selling and master its tools and techniques. Here is a guidebook for the salesman in each of us.

24. The chapter-by-chapter synopsis is effective. The synopses incorporate enough copy to show the writers' style and the substance of the book. Short synopses don't work for every book, but they work well here.

Section I—The Biggest Barrier: Fear

25 John Dowling, Executive Vice President and top sales star of Cushman & Wakefield for almost 28 years, says that he still feels fear. "Despite the bravado and the appearance of confidence, if I have to speak or do a client interview, I'm perspiring clear to my waist band. It's fear, fear of failure, fear of letting myself down, fear of letting my expectations down, fear of not being professional. No question that's my motivation. And it's a far stronger motivation than economics ever could be."

25. This concept for the opening section has a universal appeal. Every salesperson at some point has felt the potential debilitation of simple fear.

Fear is the biggest barrier to successful sales. The fear of rejection, of looking ridiculous keeps the salesperson from making the cold calls he needs to make, from meeting new clients and from closing sales.

The following chapters provide techniques for making fear work for you. By understanding the fear we all experience, you can harness fear's energy and use it to drive you to better preparation, more research and further honing of your skills.

By understanding your client's fears, you can build reassurance and confidence into the sales process. You can avoid buyer's remorse with the tools outlined in Chapter 2.

In-depth Interview. Currently Undetermined

Chapter 1—Playing the Numbers Game or Cold Calling Can Be Fun? . . . Easy? . . . Profitable?!

Our world is filled with a glorious richness of products and choices. No product or service occupies the enviable spot of being the only recognized choice to satisfy a large and growing market. Competition rises to fill any underserved niche. Without that competition, there would be no need for high priced salespeople. They could be replaced by a bank of telephone order takers.

The salesperson's first task is finding qualified candidates for his product or service. Finding the nuggets of gold at the bottom of the pan means working through more "no's" and "yes's."

The process of panning for qualified customers means cold calling and canvassing—two dreaded words in the sales world. Salespeople who learn the fine points of cold calling and who can turn the rejection involved into information take a giant step on the road to success.

26. Great lineup. This format is repeated effectively throughout the synopsis.

Tools:	Icebreakers, humor
	Scoop sheets—customer information sheets help us know what to say to build a relationship—style, interests, needs
In-depth Interview:	*Steve Dantus, Senior Managing Director, Bear Stearns.*
	Steve manages over 100 brokers and teaches his brokers how to cold call, how to recognize the only real objection they face and how to build their business. Bear Stearns' brokers average 3 to 4 times the income of brokers in other companies.
Comments:	
	Jack Kolker, Account Executive, Bear Stearns
	Art Mahony, Regional Marketing Manager, Ricoh
	Bob Benson, Field Sales Manager, Sales & Marketing Management
Cartoon:	Nine Ways to Say "No"

Chapter 2—If I Buy from You Today, Will You Respect Me Tomorrow?
Limited resources and abundant needs coupled with overwhelming choices make the life of a buyer frustrating, complex, and fearful. Many potential buyers opt out of the market or live with products or services that are not entirely satisfactory rather than deal with the anxiety of making a buying decision.

Buying a new product or service brings change and uncertainty. One of the major roles a salesperson plays is reducing that buyer's uncertainty and doubt. The minute a deal is made, the buyer is subject to buyer's remorse. The possibility of buyer's remorse can be minimized by providing him with strong examples of satisfied users and by the reassurance of a well-established buyer-salesperson relationship.

Tools: References—stories, tapes, video
                 Customer portfolios and pictures
In-depth Interviews: Bill Stack, Regional Manager, GE
                 Uses videotaped references to show satisfied users of his complex, technical product. Since beginning to use those taped references, his closing rate has improved by a minimum of 25%.

27 *John Dowling, Cushman & Wakefield*
                 Insists on having his potential clients talk to satisfied current customers. He gives them his reference list and tells them what questions to ask. He knows he will provide service beyond their expectations, but he wants them to hear that from another client rather than from him. He wants the credibility and confidence factors built into his sales process from the very beginning. He also tells new brokers how to develop this credibility and confidence when they don't have an established base of customers.

Cartoon: Recorded Customer Interviews

27. Concise anecdotes always help the reader visualize the message. More authors should, when appropriate, try to incorporate them into their proposals.

In general, this is a very well organized outline. The authors established that genuine value will be provided. It's also very well presented on an aesthetic level—an aspect that should never be neglected. A sample chapter would have been an asset, but there's enough meat here and the author credentials are strong enough to fly without one.

PROPOSAL 6

In the Beginning . . .

A Keepsake Record of Before-Birth Memories

**Written and Illustrated by
"Julie Karen"
Julie K. Walther**

This proposal is for an illustrated gift book that will include ample space for the mother-to-be to record and preserve her thoughts and feelings during pregnancy. It was purchased by Longmeadow Press, who liked the proposal so much that they asked the author to do a second book for after-birth memories.

This kind of specialized proposal requires three basic elements:

1. A clear concept that's marketable (of course it helps if there's not too much competition).
2. An author who can provide necessary graphics, artwork, and photography—or at least has access to someone who can.
3. An author with the proven ability to conceive and organize almost everything that such a book should include.

This proposal accomplished all those things, and is a perfect example of how a good idea with a strong presentation can offset an author's lack of publishing history.

1. In the original draft, the overview wasn't as direct or persuasive as it is in this rewritten version. It's now concise and clearly conveys all the pertinent information the publisher needs in order to understand the project.

2. The overview does a sufficient job of explaining the author's vision. Writing an overview for this type of book is much more challenging than for standard nonfiction books. It's difficult to categorize this book, and the editorial content is secondary to appearance and usability.

3. This overview is strong because it shows the personality of the project and generates enthusiasm. It's not written in a stuffy, formal tone. While a proposal is a sales pitch, the writing doesn't have to be strictly businesslike to be persuasive. As you read this proposal, you get a feel for the book.

4. The informality of the section headings might not work for another type of book, but it works here.

5. This section establishes the writer as an

Overview

In the Beginning is a keepsake record book for mothers who have 1 recently discovered that life as they know it will be changed forever. Pregnancy is like a rite of passage which, for most women, brings cherished memories to be shared with loved ones throughout their lives. This unique heirloom-quality record book enables mothers to easily preserve scraps, thoughts and memories which can be presented to her precious child when the time is just right.

Unlike other baby books which record the statistics, major 2 changes and accomplishments of babies as they grow, *In the Beginning* is purchased early in pregnancy and completed by the time the baby is brought home from the hospital. It captures a special time of wonder when everything is possible and full of mystery.

The format of the book includes beautifully illustrated pages for writing about the baby's life before birth—choosing names, birth-preparation classes, nursery decorating, the trip to the hospital, labor, etc., until the baby is brought home—everything that happens before the traditional "baby book" kicks in. It also includes blank pages and pockets to give freedom to each woman's individual journey. *In the Beginning* captures the variety of emotion and the brilliant spectrum of change and growth during pregnancy like no other book can. It guides the mother to express the joy and excitement, fears and frustrations—and the sometimes-comic moments—that accompany her unique pregnancy. There are pages for photos, and pockets for special items such as congratulatory notes and cards, ultrasound photos and shower invitations.

This book begins when the mother first suspects that she might 3 be pregnant and, page by page, takes her through the experience of maternity—from major events to sentimental thoughts and extraordinary feelings.

In the Beginning has the look and feel of an heirloom. It's attractive and substantial without being daunting. It's humorous, and sometimes "cute," while also being poignant and purposeful. It is approximately 60 illustrated pages in length.

Why I Am Writing This Book   4

Sixteen years ago I was pregnant with my first child. I had a strong 5 urge to keep a record of my pregnancy and attempted to do so in one of those bound, blank books. The record is sketchy, but the memories, conjured up by the few entries I did make, are precious. About a year after the birth of my daughter, I was pregnant again and, during

⁵ that pregnancy, I kept no records at all. When they became old enough, my children asked me questions about their lives before birth and greatly enjoyed hearing my earliest impressions of them. I wished that I had more to share with them than my memories.

Last year I became pregnant with my third child. Right after the test came back positive I rushed out and bought another one of those bound, blank books to write in.

But I wanted something better. That's when the idea struck me: *Mothers want to write about their child's, or children's, beginnings and a book that encourages this is desirable and valuable.*

In the Beginning meets this preexisting need!

⁶ Pregnancy is a time of introspection, acute body consciousness, intimate closeness with a person not yet seen . . . mystery and wonder! It's a time when, even though a woman may be working full time and taking care of other children, she has many quiet moments to think about the new life within her. Most women want to keep a record of their pregnancies. Doing so has immediate rewards as well as providing long-term memories to be cherished with the child, and with other family members. My older children, now 15 and 13, still love to hear me tell stories about their very earliest days.

During my recent pregnancy, I was again immersed in the spell of maternal instinct. I started *In the Beginning* while visiting doctors, getting medical tests taken, feeling the baby exercise within me, attending Lamaze classes, buying maternity clothes, reading stacks of pregnancy books, preparing a nursery, "eating for two," and living through the most amazing body changes a person can experience. *In the Beginning* is based on my own feelings and experiences.

About Me

⁷ In addition to being a mother, I am a graphic designer and artist. I have exhibited watercolors in a one-woman show, at community galleries and exhibited illustrations as a graphic arts student at UCLA. My articles on graphic design have been featured in national publications. I have designed numerous newsletters, and illustrated freelance for the past twelve years. I have taught watercolor classes to five-, six- and seven-year-old children and have given demonstrations on music and art to nursery schools. In April 1991 I began work as a volunteer to help mothers of newborns adjust to the changes and challenges of motherhood through a community outreach program sponsored by the United Way.

expert on the subject— or at least as being qualified to write the book.

6. Here the author makes a compelling statement for why this book should be published. What also counts here is the author's ability to be personal and convey poignant maternal feelings.

7. The author highlights the necessary attributes for a project of this nature: She's an accomplished graphic artist; she can write; and she's a mother who cares about other mothers. All the information is relevant to the project and shows the competence and ability necessary to the goal.

Who Will Buy This Book?

8. This strong and commonsense testimony shows that a large natural market exists for this project. This type of marketing information is useful because these ideas broaden the potential market considerably and might not have been obvious to the publisher.

In the Beginning is for mothers who have recently conceived. It's written to be reread by the parents to the child as soon as he or she asks the question, "Was I in your tummy, Mommy?" When completed, it's a written history of the child, beginning at the beginning. It will be a treasured heirloom capturing a magical time as nothing else can. **8**

Every expectant mother will want one *each time she becomes pregnant. In the Beginning* is also an ideal shower gift.

Mothers who have already given birth have excellent memories of what happened during their pregnancies. *In the Beginning* is inviting to them also and they will want to "catch up" their babies' histories and find a place for all of the treasures they have saved.

9. This observation on today's parents shows careful consideration of the book's commercial viability.

Today's parents are beginning to have babies at a later age than previous generations; most are in their 30s, many in their 40s. They are people with careers and they have money and time to invest in their children's futures. They conscientiously plan pregnancy and childbirth and cherish their family time. Many parents try for years to conceive—in the last decade fertility clinics have become very busy places. Childless celebrities say, yes, they have it all . . . except . . . a family. Babies are in vogue. *In the Beginning*'s time has come. **9**

Why People Will Buy This Book

As soon as a woman's pregnancy is confirmed, she heads to the bookstore! There are multitudes of books on what can be expected during pregnancy. There are picture books about the progression of the baby's growth in utero. There are labor and birth-preparation books. New books—about every aspect of pregnancy and birth you can imagine—are released on a regular basis.

The most closely related books to *In the Beginning* are *The Pregnancy Organizer* by Pamela Eisenberg, and *Pregnancy Day By Day* by Sheila Kitzinger. *The Pregnancy Organizer* is in small looseleaf-binder form and like a Day Timer® in purpose—organizing and planning. *Pregnancy Day By Day* is primarily an informational book with small spaces to write about various aspects of pregnancy. While *In the Beginning* has a slight similarity to these books, it is in a class by itself. It's the only book that focuses on the life of the child before birth—ultimately to share the experience with the child.

There are no pregnancy-related books designed to begin a child's history before birth. So many things happen at the very beginning of life that are lost to posterity without *In the Beginning*.

There are no pregnancy-related books designed to share with your child. *In the Beginning* has room for the mother to write all that she wants to express to her son or daughter. There are lovely illustrations, timeless in quality, as appropriate now as they will be in 25 years.

In the Beginning is unique because it's not just a diary; it gives the mother the opportunity to do much more than just make journal entries. *In the Beginning* is a fertile place, bringing life to the thoughts and details of the mother's entries.

There is nothing like it currently available. It's such a simple idea that when people see it they will say, "Why hasn't someone thought of that before?"

Marketability/Promotion

10 There is a place for *In the Beginning* in all bookstores, card and gift shops and stationery stores. Maternity and parenting magazines (*9 Months, Parenting, American Baby, Child, Childbirth*) are ideal for reviews and advertising. Hospital gift shops, especially those in hospitals that offer birth-preparation classes, are also appropriate outlets. Birthing-class instructors will help promote it to attending parents-to-be.

11 TV shows such as "The Home Show" and "Live With Regis & Kathie Lee" are ideal forums for promotion.

Timing

In the Beginning will be completed within eight months of my signing a contract with the publisher.

12 ## Sample Page Subjects

Opening Poem

13 ### First Inklings*
I first thought that I might be pregnant when . . .
I decided to get a positive answer . . .
When I told your Dad, he . . .
What our friends said . . .
And our families . . .
I felt . . .

News Traveled Fast*
We got congratulations from . . .
And phone calls from . . .
*Marked pages are illustrated on accompanying art boards.

10. The marketability and promotion section shows some innovative ideas. The publishing house might not have thought in terms of the gift market and birth preparation classes.

11. This section's weakness is that there is no indication of the author's ability to promote the book through these avenues. While the ideas are good, there is no practical link between the author and the promotions.

12. This outline presentation shows strong and comprehensive organization. Every emotion and event relevant to the experience appear to be addressed. It's evident that this book will be a real tool for the reader to express and record intimate feelings.

13. Including these poems helps set the "from-the-heart" tone the book will have.

Here are some of the special wishes that were sent . . .

Pocket

About Your Mom
I was born
What was happening that year
Stories I liked as a child
Games I played
Pets I had
About my family

About Your Dad
He was born
What was happening that year
His favorite stories
His favorite games
His pets
His family

Doctor Visits
Your estimated time of arrival was . . .
Routine tests
Ultrasound (photo if available)
Special tests (when and why)
When I first heard your heartbeat . . .

Getting a Kick out of You*
I felt the first flutter . . .
You wriggled regularly by . . .
When your movements were stronger, it felt like . . .
Sometimes I wondered if . . .
When your Dad first felt you move with his hand, he . . .

Keeping Busy
At work
At play
While waiting I made you a . . .
Trips I took while pregnant

Diet & Health (2 pages)
I had some crazy cravings . . .
And some favorite treats were . . .

You were worth the weight! I gained . . .
My favorite exercise was . . .
Just before you were born my waist measured . . .

Poem

Photo page

Education
I went to birth-preparation classes at . . .
I learned . . .
The classes made me feel . . .
Books that I read . . .

Wishes and Dreams
Poem

Good dreams/scary dreams
Wishes and hopes

Letters to Our Child
From Mother
From Father

Pockets

The Name Game (2 pages)
Name books I read . . .
Girls' names I liked . . .
        Top five names . . .
Boys' names I liked . . .
        Top five names . . .
The final decision . . .
Why we chose to name you _____

Shopping (2 pages)
Maternity clothes, my favorite ones
Preparing your layette . . .

Your Nursery
Planning and doing
Colors and characters

Photo of your nursery

Shower Time*
Where . . .
When . . .
Gifts for you . . .
Who came . . .

Photo page

Pocket for invitation and cards

Dazed Days
One day I was so clumsy I . . .
One of the funniest things that happened . . .
Sometimes when I couldn't get up . . .

Hospital Preparation
Packing the bag
Practice run
Touring the nursery

Labor and Delivery (2 pages)
False starts
The real thing—when/where
I was in labor (how long) . . .
Who was there to share . . .
To feel comfortable I brought . . .
My thoughts and feelings . . .

On Your Mark, Get Set, You!
Just one look
First hug
Dad's impressions

Your first photo

Special Pockets (2)
ID bracelet
Dad's hospital mask
Bassinet card

Vital Statistics
Weight
Length
Hair, eyes, etc.

Closing Poem

Opening Poem
Your life begins as does a rose
A seed is planted, then it grows
With love and caring, a bud appears
And flowers bloom throughout the years
As the rose began beneath the earth
Our love began before your birth

Health & Diet page
Even when I was tired
At the end of a long day
I always felt happpy
That you were on the way

Dreams Poem
"As long as you're healthy. . ." I've often said
As long as you're warm and loved and fed
As long as you smile then I'll smile too
With my hopes fulfilled and
My dreams come true

Closing Poem
We were together quite a while
Before we really met
And the moment I first saw you
Is one I won't forget
And through the weeks and months and years
I'll keep open my ears and my heart
And let you know I've loved you so
Right from the very start

The following sample pages are important because they show off the author's creative and artistic talents—which are of primary importance for this kind of book. The sample pages also provide an exact visualization of how the project will be executed; they bring everything to life and prove the project's workability.

Getting a Kick Out of You

I felt the first flutter _____

_____

You wiggled regularly by _____

_____

When your movements were stronger it felt like _____

_____

_____

Sometimes I wondered if _____

_____

What your Dad thought when he first felt you move _____

_____

_____

_____

_____

_____

Shower Time

A shower was held for us!

When _____

Where _____

Friends who came _____

_____

_____

_____

_____

_____

Family who came _____

_____

_____

_____

Gifts received _____

_____

_____

_____

_____

_____

121

PROPOSAL 7

"I'm Too Young to Have a Heart Attack"

by
Jim Castelli

This proposal was originally sold to Prima Publishing and came out in 1990 as a hardcover—with this title. The book was then republished by Prima in 1992 in a quality paperback format with a new title: *There's Life After a Heart Attack: A Journalist's Life Affirming Account of Recovery.* It was believed that the new title would broaden the book's appeal beyond strictly "young" heart-disease victims.

Several publishers expressed strong interest in this book proposal for two reasons: (1) Heart-disease books tend to sell well; and (2) this is an excellent proposal by an author who has experienced heart disease and has impressive credentials as a journalist.

I. Synopsis

Each year, 1.5 million Americans have heart attacks; one in 20 is [1] under the age of 40. Cardiologists report that the average age of heart attack victims is getting younger. "Family Ties," one of the most-watched programs on television, built a three-part episode around the heart attack of Steven Keaton, the quintessential Baby-Boomer. Most of the ads selling low-cholesterol, low-fat products are aimed at people in their 30s and 40s.

The Baby Boomers are worried about heart attacks—and I have [2] a lot to tell them about how to avoid one and how to recover from one. In 1985, at the age of 38, I had a massive heart attack and was not expected to leave the emergency room alive. Within a few months, I was living a full, productive life and was in the best physical shape of my life; that remains the case today.

While I was beginning my recovery in the hospital, my wife [3] combed stores for books to help me adjust to my new life. Many were useful—they helped explain what had happened to me; they described the role of diet, exercise and stress reduction in preventing another attack. But none provided what I needed most, a short, upbeat but realistic account of recovery from a heart attack by someone who had been through the experience himself; and it would have helped even more if that someone had been part of my own generation. I knew that I had to somehow change my entire life, yet not lose myself in the process; no guide to counting cholesterol can teach you how to do that.

I want to write the book I desperately needed to read—and that [4] my wife needed to read—while I was in the hospital. *I'm Too Young to Have a Heart Attack* will be that book, a short, readable, practical account of a heart attack and its aftermath by someone who's been there, written in an informal, conversational style.

I'll provide important information about the mechanics and logistics of a heart attack and recovery. But, much more importantly, I'll tell my readers—primarily young heart attack victims and their families—what was going on in my mind as well as what was going on in my body. I knew I was in fight mode; I just didn't know how or who to fight. I also knew that, as with any serious illness, having the right attitude could spell the difference between surviving—or not.

Most of this story will be important to people of any age who are concerned about heart attack. But it is of particular interest to other Baby Boomers.

Several major themes will run through *I'm Too Young to Have a Heart Attack*.

---

1. This scene-setting paragraph offers a solid statistic relevant to the book's market. The market for health books is always competitive, but the author convincingly points out that a sizeable target market exists and is still available for this book. He also shows there's a high level of popular consciousness about the proposed book's subject.

2. This paragraph lets us know in a powerful way why we should listen to this author.

3. We saw this proposal at an earlier stage when the tone was more distant. In this version, the thesis paragraph is written in a personal style that's much more appropriate for this type of book. In the following paragraphs, the writer shows a vulnerability that was sorely missed in the first draft. The style of the synopsis gives the editor a sense of how the book will be written.

4. This paragraph explains clearly why the book should exist and why this author is the best "expert" for the job—one of the things an editor looks for when deciding whether to acquire a book.

5 ■ *The Baby-Boomer Angle.* There are significant differences in the challenges facing someone who has a heart attack at 58 and someone who has one at 38. I had a young wife, Jayne, two children—Matt, 14, and Dan, 6—and only 27 years left on a 30-year mortgage.

■ *Perspective.* Recovery is a lifelong process requiring constant vigilance. After a heart attack, you go through cycles. The immediate reaction is shock. This is followed by exhilaration—something like what people feel when they've been shot at and missed. Next comes a mixture of determination and apprehension; you work to recover, but worry whether or not you will. After a few months, there's a "return to normalcy" that can be both your best friend and your worst enemy; you need to feel "normal" in order to recover, but if you fall back into your old lifestyle, you can endanger your health again. "Normal" becomes a series of swings between backsliding and recommitment.

6   As I write this, my heart itself is in better shape than that of the average man my age who has not had a heart attack, my blood pressure is normal and I have a resting pulse rate of 60; at the same time, I can't seem to get either my weight or my cholesterol levels down to stay and I haven't found a magic answer for dealing with stress. It's a constant fight. You don't really know that in the rosy glow of the first few months after an attack.

7 ■ *Self-Help.* Doctors saved my life but—and the system is set up this way—it was primarily nonphysicians who played the major role in educating me and helping me to adjust. Family members, nurses, the people running a cardiac rehabilitation program, a social worker, and, most significantly, other heart attack victims provided the information, insight and support that was essential to a full recovery. In addition to emphasizing this theme in the narrative, I will include an appendix with a unique directory of resources for cardiac self-help across the country.

I'm Too Young to Have a Heart Attack will include 50,000 words of narrative plus appendices. It will contain a Foreword written by James A. Metcalf, Ph.D., exercise physiologist for the Northern Virginia Cardiac Therapy Program of Fairfax Hospital and associate professor of health and leisure studies at George Mason University.

---

5. Here the author begins to explain why his unique perspective needs to be presented. It's a good tactic to delineate your themes in this way.

**6. This passage is excellent. Many books try to have all the answers; this author says he has some of the answers but that he still has problems, too. This realistic approach to the subject gives the author credibility and shows that the book will be useful and not filled with fluff.

**7. It's always helpful for a nonfiction project to offer something tangible to the reader. This appendix is a useful addition and selling point. It also shows how well focused this book proposal is.

8. The marketing section does a sufficient job of explaining why this book has commercial potential. A strong sell isn't necessary here. The publishers and editors who received this proposal were aware of the subject—especially as it relates to book sales. The author just had to reinforce the obvious, while avoiding the inadvertent introduction of any negatives.

9. Some of this information would be obvious to the publisher. However, the concept of spouses of heart attack victims as a secondary market is innovative, as is the idea of targeting hospital gift shops specifically among sales outlets.

10. The possibilities for magazine exposure would be stronger if the author could identify direct contacts. Promotion ideas are more impressive if they're supported by the author's credentials. If you have the contacts, state them directly.

11. The author doesn't mention experience with radio or television formats, perhaps leading an editor to dismiss these statements as fluff or wishful thinking.

12. The author was wise to acknowledge the competition. He then states effectively why he

II. Marketing and Promotion

The primary audience for *I'm Too Young to Have a Heart Attack* is composed of everyone under the age of 50 who has a heart attack in a given year. There are several secondary audiences: heart attack victims of any age; health-conscious Baby Boomers; anyone who is concerned about heart attacks because they have risk factors such as high cholesterol, coronary artery disease or high blood pressure. A key market is composed of the spouses of heart attack victims; while not all heart attack victims are men, most are, and it is appropriate to think in terms of their wives as a receptive market. [8]

This book could appear in the health or nonfiction sections of virtually every general bookstore in the country. Other potential outlets include hospital gift shops, health and fitness stores and, of course, libraries. [9]

In addition to the normal book-review opportunities, *I'm Too Young to Have a Heart Attack* should get exposure in men's magazines, women's magazines, and health and fitness publications. [10]

The topic is a natural for discussion on radio and TV talk shows, particularly on local stations and cable. It also offers feature story opportunities for print. [11]

There are special opportunities, due to local interest, in the populous Northern Virginia area where I live and was treated; Fairfax County alone, for example, has a population the size of San Francisco's. Local print and broadcast stories should generate publicity and sales.

III. Competition

While there are many heart-related books on the market today, there are none which combine the elements in *I'm Too Young to Have a Heart Attack*. Most books are by M.D.s and involve medical advice. Many focus on one dimension, such as cholesterol. *The Healing Heart* by Norman Cousins is about an older man and includes barely a mention of his family. *Mr King, You're Having a Heart Attack* by Larry King is primarily a celebrity book which, again, describes a more classic heart attack patient; it was also written within a few months of his attack. People I've talked with in the Northern Virginia Cardiac Rehab program say they know of no other book like the one I propose. [12]

IV. Credentials

In this case, the best credential is firsthand experience. But my 20 years as a journalist also qualify me to write this book. My background [13]

13 has trained me to write for a popular audience and to convey a great deal of information in a small space in an easily understandable manner. The word that has been used more than any other to describe my style is simply "readable." I can guarantee a narrative tone that is neither too personal nor too clinical, and I know how to tell an individual story that has broad appeal.

14   My previous books are *The Bishops and the Bomb: Waging Peace in a Nuclear Age* (Doubleday, 1983); *The American Catholic People: Their Beliefs, Practices and Values*, with George Gallup, Jr. (Doubleday, 1987); *The Emerging Parish: The Notre Dame Study of Catholic Life Since Vatican II*, with Joseph Gremillion (Harper & Row, 1988); *A Plea for Common Sense: Resolving the Clash Between Religion and Politics* (Harper & Row, 1988). *The People's Religion: American Faith in the '90s* with George Gallup will be published by Macmillan in Fall, 1989.

    My experience includes serving as Religion Editor for *The Washington Star* and a part-time correspondent for *Time* and *People* magazines. I currently write a religion column for Gannett News Service and the Gallup Religion Poll with George Gallup, Jr. My articles and columns, including several humor pieces, have appeared in *The Washington Post, The Los Angeles Times, The Chicago Tribune, The Miami Herald, The Boston Globe, The Atlanta Constitution, The Baltimore Evening Sun, USA Today* and other publications.

V. Outline

FOREWORD by James A. Metcalf.

INTRODUCTION. In this brief section, I will situate the reader for the beginning of the narrative. (ATTACHED).

15 **Chapter I: Heart Attack.** This chapter will describe the events leading up to my heart attack, the attack itself, and my four days in the Coronary Care Unit, the cardiac intensive care unit. (ATTACHED).

Chapter II: Recuperation and Reeducation. This section will describe my six days in the Progressive Care Unit, the recovery unit where cardiac patients are sent once they are out of danger. During this period, I began recuperation (including physical therapy) and reeducation, learning about everything from the physiology of heart attacks to diet, exercise, medication and further medical procedures including angiograms, angioplasty and by-passes.

has something of value to contribute to the existing body of knowledge. However, in this case—when there are so many books about the subject—the competition section should have greater emphasis. It might be wise to make a title-by-title comparison with specific examples of how this book can be distinguished from each of its rivals.

13. Publishing credits are great if you have them, but in nonfiction, credible expertise in the subject area and a mastery of the English language in a clear and readable writing style may be enough. The author shows he has a strong combination of both and presents this confidently and coherently.

14. This author's publishing credits happen to be exceptional, but his prolific book-writing career could have been presented with greater impact. Each book title should have been entered on a separate line, prefaced by a bullet for impact.

15. This is a strong outline because it's sequentially organized and provides plenty of well-written elaboration. The author demonstrates a solid vision, legitimate voice, and the requisite skills to write this book. It might have been useful to place a skeletal

table of contents before this detailed outline so the editor could see the game plan before approaching the detail.

This chapter will answer a series of questions: What is a heart attack? What causes it? What are the prospects for recovery? How do you prevent a heart attack? Does cutting back on cholesterol mean that I can never eat another cheeseburger? When is surgery required, and what are the options? What medications are available? What can exercise do? What about sex after a heart attack? (One of the many brochures they gave me in the hospital was entitled "The Sensuous Heart," a cartoon-style presentation designed to make you relax about sex. The major guideline the staff offered was that you were ready for sex when you could walk up two flights of stairs without losing your breath—and they made me walk up two flights of stairs before they would discharge me.)

During this period, the psychological readjustment begins, although the hospital stay itself acts as a buffer; there's a survival euphoria, your friends all come to visit, you don't worry about things like whether the car payment got mailed on time, and nurses bring you milk and cookies and rub your back at bedtime. You know there's work ahead and it starts to take shape in your mind, but the hard part doesn't really begin until you go home.

Chapter III: Going Home. This will cover about two-and-a-half months after I came home from the hospital. This is the most difficult time for most cardiac patients, because that's when the reality hits—you're back in a familiar environment that doesn't feel quite the same anymore.

The most common feeling during this period is apprehension: I worried about how I would live my day-to-day life, work, adjust to a new diet and exercise program, deal with the pressures on my wife and kids, who were still in a state of shock.

The approach of the major turning points in this period all produce anxiety: at one month after the heart attack, you take a modified stress test to determine whether you can resume driving and having sexual relations (I don't drive); at about five weeks after the attack, you have an angiogram which assesses the extent of damage and determines whether surgery—angioplasty or by-pass—is necessary; at about eight weeks afterward, you take a treadmill stress test to determine how well your heart is functioning.

** (This section in particular will be greatly expanded and integrated over a longer period:)

My exercise program called for me to begin walking a quarter of a mile a day as soon as I got home from the hospital and to gradually increase my distance and speed. By the time I had my angiogram, I was walking about a mile and a half a day at faster than 4 miles an hour. The angiogram results read like a good news, bad news joke. The good news was that another heart attack was highly unlikely. One of my cardiologists, Dr. Marder, explained that while doctors talk about three arteries, in about 40 percent of the population, the right artery was practically vestigial, serving no real purpose, while the left artery was about double normal size and, in effect, did double duty. That was my situation. The anterior artery, where the attack occurred, was completely blocked, as was the tiny right artery. The left artery, however, was "clean as a whistle"—no blockages at all. (Jayne and I immediately dubbed this "Super-Artery.")

The bad news was that the angiogram revealed a ventricular aneurysm—a flap of tissue which had survived in the damaged area. This aneurysm would use blood without doing me any good. Dr. Marder painted a bleak picture about the limits this would put on me—"If you play softball with your kids, you won't be able to run to first base." I tried to explain that I had walked almost two miles at a fast clip the day before without any problems, but it didn't sink in. By the time I left the hospital, I thought I was looking at life as a cripple, and a short life at that.

I called Marder that night and got a more optimistic reading—doctors never like to commit themselves to anything definite, good or bad. I went back to my walking. A few weeks later, Dan fell off his bike and cut himself and Jayne and I took him to the emergency room—the one where I'd had my attack. As we were leaving, we ran into Dr. Bhushan, the internist who had treated me in the hospital. He had received the angiogram results and—thinking he was helping me—told me my age made me an excellent candidate for a heart transplant. I practically fainted; Jayne looked up to see me stretched out on a cot to get my equilibrium back.

But I walked some more—and some more. Finally, the day of truth came—I took the full treadmill test nine weeks after my attack. The test was designed to determine my maximum heart rate, which, at my age, should have been 180 for a healthy man. As I walked on the treadmill, I watched Dr. Herron's reactions as he monitored the readings. The expression "the eyes bulged out of his head" is a cliché, but this was the first time I ever saw it literally happen; I could tell he didn't believe how well I was doing. "Take it easy, you've got nothing to prove," he said. "Bullshit," I thought, but I didn't say it because I'd already complained to him about the other doctors' pessimism.

After nine minutes on the treadmill, at increasing speeds and higher inclines, my pulse rate reached 180 and he stopped the test. I was clearly in better shape than anyone—anyone except me, that is—expected. When I started my cardiac rehab program a few weeks later, the nurse in charge looked at the record of the treadmill test, looked up and said, "This is the test of an average man your age who hasn't had a heart attack."

Appendices

16. Appendices are often valuable bonuses, or throw-ins. Such reference material can help the reader begin to apply whatever he or she has learned from the book.

In addition to the material published here, the author provided an introduction and a long first chapter. The well-written and extensive sample material gave editors confidence that this author would prove capable once signed. Even though the author has strong book and magazine credits, this book was a departure from his usual editorial specialties. In a way, he had to prove himself from scratch. We might have sold this project even without the samples—but probably for at least 25 percent less.

A. Self-Help Directory. This will be a unique listing of cardiac self-[16] help centers across the country. In assembling it, I will begin with a list of every American Heart Association affiliate in the country and add other sources I obtain from these affiliates and other sources.

B. Diet. A brief summary of basic information on calories, fat and cholesterol in common foods.

C. Exercise. Similarly, this will include some very basic information on exercise, including how many calories are burned off by different exercises.

D. Bibliography. An annotated bibliography commenting on the usefulness of some popular heart-related books.

E. Medical Update. Some "news brief" type reports on new medical studies related to heart disease.

Index. For medical issues.

PROPOSAL 8

Workstyles to Fit Your Lifestyle

The Hands-On Guide to Temporary Employment

by
John Fanning
and
Rosemary Maniscalco

This proposal is for a career book. Three publishers made offers for it, and it was sold to Prentice Hall, largely because two top honchos from the business books division made a special trip to the authors' offices to explain why PH would be the best publisher.

Publishers don't often fight for books in that way. But this one had some special things going for it:

1. The primary author is the founder and CEO of a multimillion-dollar publicly traded company with more than 100 franchised offices.
2. The company promised to purchase approximately 10,000 units of the book—a volume that makes even the largest publishers rather happy.
3. The company had an effective public relations firm on retainer to promote the book.

Don't get the wrong idea—you don't need such impressive credentials to sell a proposal. If the authors hadn't had so much going for them the book may have been published, but the advance would have been significantly lower, and it's unlikely that personal visits would have been made to the authors. Although it's not indicated anywhere in this proposal,

131

the project has a ghost-writer. It can't hurt to mention this in a proposal, especially if it's an impressive ghost.

1. The title of the book seems clumsy, although its subtitle is just right. Something like "Work to Fit Your Lifestyle" might have been a better choice. This bold first paragraph immediately states the need for the book, how the authors plan to fill it, and what the book's thesis will be.

2. Another effective way to begin this overview would be to reverse the two opening paragraphs. The first paragraph would then feature this impressive statistic that supports the viability of temping as an employment option that has been until now a "well kept secret."

3. If the subject matter of your book is a little dry, be sure to put your aces up front to keep the editor reading. The author's use of these bullets is effective because it helps the editor visualize the various people who will benefit from the book and generates immediate enthusiasm.

This information could have been saved for the marketing section. However, there are no absolute laws about proposal writing. Do what you think will work so you can secure a contract.

Overview

There is currently no book that shows people how to take advantage [1] of the growing number of rewarding career opportunities now available in the temporary help industry. *Workstyles to Fit Your Lifestyle* fills that gap by providing all the tools and information readers need to earn money temping, while satisfying their short- and long-term career and lifestyle objectives.

Once the primary domain of fill-in secretaries and people out-of- [2] work, temping is now a viable option for some 10 million women and men in virtually every industry and professional field. Temporary employment provides unmatched flexibility, as well as a number of unique challenges and career opportunities. It is a particularly desirable choice for people who can identify with one or more of the following statements:

- I prefer working only when it suits my needs and wants. [3]
- I am between positions and need to have money coming in.
- I am a wife and mother who wants to supplement my family's income.
- I am a recent college graduate seeking an entry-level position in a competitive field.
- I am a retired person who wants to remain active and productive.
- I'd like to join the ranks of those who have turned a temporary job into a permanent position.
- I've been out of the job market for a number of years, and would like to ease my way back and update my skills.
- I am a performing or creative artist who requires flexibility and extra income.

Coauthor John Fanning is the founder and president of [4] Uniforce Temporary Services, Inc.—a nationally franchised temporary employment service with offices coast to coast.

Mr. Fanning is a nationally known expert on the temporary services field. He has appeared on such TV programs as "The MacNeil/Lehrer News Hour", and has been featured in articles in *Forbes* and *Business Week* magazines.

Coauthor Rosemary Maniscalco is executive vice president of Uniforce, and a member of its board of directors. Ms. Maniscalco started as a temp and worked her way up through the ranks. Today, she is one of the few female executives to achieve top management status for a major temporary service in the United States. She has been interviewed on numerous radio programs, including "The Barry Farber Show", and has been featured in magazine articles in such publications as *Working Woman* and *The Office*.

Mr. Fanning and Ms. Maniscalco have led this publicly held company to a position of national prominence. In separate articles, *Business Week* ranked Uniforce as one of the best small companies in the U.S., and cited it among six of "franchising's hot performers."

In explaining why the temporary industry is now America's second fastest-growing service business, the authors cite five trends:

5
1. In today's mobile society, more people either require or prefer flexible work hours.
2. The demand for skilled personnel is expanding at a much faster rate than the available labor force.
6
3. There are an estimated 14 million nonworking women caring for their families at home, and over 3 million men and women who have taken early retirement.* Members of these two large groups are filling an increasing number of the jobs that will continue to become available throughout the 1990s. Temping offers the most practical and comfortable way for many of these individuals to enter or reenter the workforce.
4. The automation of the office has created a need for personnel who can operate computerized equipment on a multitude of software packages. Temporary services are adept at meeting corporate America's growing demand for employees with these and other highly specialized skills.
7
5. Using temporary help makes it easier for businesses to control hiring, training and benefits costs, thus enabling them to protect their profit margins.

The authors' primary objective in writing *Workstyles to Fit Your Lifestyle* is to show readers how to navigate the changing currents of today's temporary employment industry. Mr. Fanning and Ms. Maniscalco supplement their collective personal and professional experience with insights and anecdotes from a large cross-section of their franchisees, temporary employees and corporate clients. Checklists, interview tips and self-evaluation materials are included throughout the chapters to give readers everything they need to:

8
- Realistically assess their marketable skills.
- Select a service that can best address their needs.

---

* Source: *Megatrends 2000*

4. Another example of not holding off until the traditional sequential position to inject a sales point. The authors have excellent credentials, and the ghostwriter wanted the editor to know this immediately. (A full bio section does follow.)

5. Concise and pertinent supporting evidence. The authors are building a very persuasive case with each sentence. There's no fluff here.

6. It helps greatly to support the book's thesis with documented facts and figures organized numerically.

7. This statement indicates that business may be a potentially substantial secondary market for the book—or perhaps indicates a need for a follow-up book geared specifically toward businesses.

8. This indicates that the book will include a practical program in addition to its other claims—a must for any commercial book of this nature.

- Maximize earnings.
- Build in such perks as health benefits and vacations.
- Design a personalized temporary-employment game plan.

Market Analysis

9. The author tackles the competition head on and makes a strong positive statement in favor of the proposed book. He starts out by showing the competition is slight, which may cause an editor to think that "where there are no books there is no market." The author anticipates this possibility and gives many reasons why it would be a wrong conclusion.

An extensive search of resources, including *Books In Print*, turned up [9] only three books on the topic of temporary employment: John Fanning's *Work When You Want to Work*, originally published by Collier Macmillan in 1969 and reprinted in 1985 by Pocket Books; *Temp Worker's Handbook* by Lewis & Nancy Schuman, published by The American Management Association (AMACOM); and *Professional Temping* by Eve Broudy, published by Collier Macmillan.

10. When referring to another book by the author of this proposed project, it would have been persuasive to point out that he is a pioneer in the field. The author chose to treat this information as he would any competition—a missed opportunity.

Of these three books, Mr. Fanning's *Work When You Want to Work* [10] is the only one to give readers a complete guide to temping. It is clear, however, that a new book is needed—one that shows readers how to take advantage of the dramatic changes that have reshaped the temporary help industry.

Today, the pay scale, benefits and training opportunities in some areas of temporary employment have reached the point where thousands of people are declining permanent positions in favor of career temping. Recent articles and industry surveys reveal the following trends:

11. These facts and figures effectively show that the book has commercial potential.

- Nine out of ten American businesses use temporary help. [11] There are now almost 10 million temporary employees in an industry that has grown by an average of 18.9 percent a year since 1970 (U.S. Department of Labor statistics).
- The use of temporary help is proving to be a highly cost-efficient measure in tight economic times. There has also been an improvement in the quality and the range of services offered by temporary services (*Managers Magazine*).
- Temps are now used by small businesses as well as Fortune 500 companies. An estimated 944,000 temps work each week through some ten thousand temporary services. When asked what attracts them to temping, these men and women cite flexible schedules, extra income and the ability to sample work environments in various businesses (*The Office*).
- Professions that are especially promising now for people seeking temporary employment include law, healthcare, computers and technical fields (*Nation's Business*).

12 In view of the rapid expansion of the temporary industry and recent economic trends, the proposed book is one that will be useful to a large readership. The number of women and men who will consider temping as a short- or long-range career option in the next few years can be measured in seven-figure terms. These potential readers will need the kind of timely information contained in *Workstyles to Fit Your Lifestyle*.

12. This statement is eyecatching.

Voice and Scope

13 The authors plan to write a 50-60,000 word self-help book in a readable, straightforward style. The chapters will be targeted toward readers who are considering temping as an interim or permanent career option. The materials will also be useful for those who already have temping experience.

The discussion will begin with an overview of the temporary employment industry, and an exploration of the basics of successful temping. The chapters will emphasize those opportunities and trends that are likely to have the greatest impact on readers throughout the 1990s and into the twenty-first century. *Workstyles to Fit Your Lifestyle* is the only book that helps readers answer the following questions:

14
- What are the most sought-after and highest-paying temp job skills?
- Why are more people choosing to become career temps?
- When is temping the most practical way to secure a desirable permanent position?
- Why do opportunities for temps increase during a recession?
- Why is temping ideally suited to our mobile society?
- Why is temping the best way for homemakers and retirees to enter or reenter the workplace?

13. This "Voice and Scope" section is usually referred to as "the format." Many proposals skip this altogether, but it's a good idea to state somewhere what your plans are for the book, such as word count. Don't characterize your book as "self-help" if it may limit your market. Sometimes the publishers can best make these types of decisions.

14. This listing gives another good overview of the book's substance, but this section is not entirely necessary, as the editor will shortly be evaluating the chapter-by-chapter outline.

Throughout the chapters, readers will be shown how to customize the information to suit their particular needs. Sample interview questions and skill-assessment tests will be included to help readers prepare for interviews and job assignments.

Firsthand anecdotes and practical advice will help readers navigate unexpected or difficult situations. Time management, financial planning and other self-evaluation tools will help readers pinpoint and realize their career and lifestyle goals.

Readers will finish the book with a good understanding of the opportunities in temporary employment, an assessment of how well suited they are to take advantage of these opportunities and a personalized temporary-employment game plan.

Sales and Promotion

15. The statement "prepared to purchase a significant number of books. . ." makes an editor's antennae stand at attention. If you are able to buy a large number of books and will sign a contract to that effect, you will have substantially more leverage in obtaining a contract and a sizeable advance. A "significant" buyback usually begins in the 5,000-unit range, which is why only a few authors are ready to commit to one.

16. It's beneficial to provide actual publicity "news hooks," or story ideas, in this section. This shows some creativity. It's also a good idea to place relevant media experience with this information.

17. These impressive bio sketches show that the authors have all the requisite credentials to write and promote this book. In this case, though, there was much more that should have been included. For example, The Uniforce Company is publicly traded on the NASDAQ; Uniforce has more than 100 franchise offices throughout the country; it's one of the top ten temp agencies;

John Fanning and Rosemary Maniscalco are an especially strong marketing team. Upon the release of *Workstyles to Fit Your Lifestyle*, the authors will work with the publisher in launching a multifaceted advertising and promotional campaign. To bolster bookstore sales, Uniforce is prepared to purchase a significant number of books to be distributed through its national network of offices. [15]

Workstyles to Fit Your Lifestyle will be an outstanding promotional tool for both print and electronic media exposure. These are some of the timely issues the authors are prepared to address on interviews and panel discussions: [16]

- How to generate more income during tough economic times.
- What it's like to work as a temp.
- How temping is smoothing the path for some 14 million women who are entering or reentering the workplace in record numbers.
- Rewarding second-career opportunities for retired persons.
- Unusual workstyles in changing times.
- The new breed of temps: physicians, attorneys, executives, computer experts.
- Successful people in business and the arts who've worked as temps.

About the Authors

John Fanning, founder and president of Uniforce Temporary Services, is a nationally recognized innovator in the personnel field. Mr. Fanning's pioneering efforts in the industry began in 1954, when at the age of 23, he founded the Fanning Personnel Agency in New York City. In 1966, Mr. Fanning sold his interest in this highly successful operation to devote his time to building the Uniforce network. The company now has franchise offices nationwide. [17]

Mr. Fanning is one of the most visible and articulate spokespersons in the temporary services field. He is the author of *Work When You Want to Work* (Pocket), and is extensively quoted in the book *Work Smart Not Hard* (Facts on File).

Mr. Fanning is regularly featured in newspapers and national publications, such as *Business Week* and *Forbes*. He has been interviewed on such TV programs as "The MacNeil/Lehrer News Hour" and "The Long Island Report" as well as on numerous radio talk shows.

Rosemary Maniscalco, executive vice president of Uniforce Temporary Services, is a dynamic corporate executive, as well as an articulate and attractive public speaker. Ms. Maniscalco joined Uniforce's marketing department in 1981. She rose rapidly through the ranks to become director of corporate development in 1983. The author was promoted to her present position in 1984. To this day, she remains one of the few female executives to hold a top management position for a major temporary service in the United States.

Ms. Maniscalco is primarily involved in the growth and development of the Uniforce's national franchise network. She has also been instrumental in creating Uniforce's innovative training and educational programs. Her creative vision is key to the success of Uniforce's national advertising and public relations campaigns with the trade, business and consumer media.

Ms. Maniscalco has been featured in magazine articles in such publications as *Working Woman* and *The Office*, and has been interviewed on numerous radio programs, including "The Barry Farber Show."

[18] # Chapter Synopsis

Workstyles to Fit Your Lifestyle
The Hands-On Guide to Temporary Employment
by John Fanning and Rosemary Maniscalco

[19] # Table of Contents

---

and it's been a top performer on the Inc. 500. This information was included in collateral support materials but would also have been effective in the body of the proposal. Don't count on the editors reading your entire package cover to cover. There's a piece missing: The book is being ghost-written by Gene Busnar, a New York based writer who has collaborated or authored more than a dozen nonfiction books. His impressive background should have been included.

18. Editors and agents greatly appreciate a comprehensive synopsis/outline like this one. There's enough material here to prove that the book will provide good information, and the expansive sample chapter that accompanied this proposal eliminated the "but can he write?" feelings editors often have.

19. It's always a good idea to have a separate table of contents before the chapter synopses. This one appears to be just right. This title for Chapter Nine could raise a few eyebrows. It's too undefined. Otherwise, the table of contents shows logic and is a good blueprint for the book.

CHAPTER ONE: Temporary Services: The Field That's Always Hiring

20. The entries in this bulleted list place emphasis on the advantages for people who temp. Always make your outline conform to your projected market.

The authors introduce themselves, and share with readers vital infor-[20] mation about the expanding opportunities in the temporary employment industry. Several recent success stories are described briefly. These include:

- Mark, a recent college graduate, who was offered a permanent position as a junior copywriter by an advertising agency after a three-week temporary assignment.
- Ruth, a forty-six-year-old mother of two college-age children who had not been gainfully employed for fifteen years, was anxious about reentering the workplace. Temping gave her the opportunity to earn money, improve her skills and gain confidence.
- Sam, an accountant who took early retirement at age fifty-five, returned to the workplace as a temp after three years of relative inactivity, and now feels more needed and respected than ever before.
- Liz, an aspiring dancer, possesses word processing skills that have enabled her to make a comfortable living as a career temp.
- Phil, age fifty, was fired after eleven years as a middle manager at a major communications company. Temping made it possible for him to generate income while exploring career possibilities at several companies.

The authors proceed to explain how the temporary employment industry operates:

Temporary help firms are paid by businesses to find and screen qualified employees. The client company pays an hourly service charge for each employee placed. There is never a charge to the temporary employee. The service makes its profit by marking up the hourly wage it pays its employees.

More and more businesses are finding that the hourly rate charged by temp services is offset by the savings in recruitment costs, fringe benefits, severance pay, worker's compensation and unemployment insurance—all of which are handled by the temporary service. Qualified temporary employees have the advantage of being able to work when they want at a competitive rate of pay, while avoiding the time and drudgery of job hunting.

Temporary employees are, in effect, working for the temporary service—not for the company to which they report. It is the temp service that hires, fires, and withholds taxes and social security. Depending on the service, employees may be offered opportunities for training, vacations and other fringe benefits.

Temporary help services recruit new employees through advertising, word of mouth—and by offering bonuses to current employees for bringing new temps into the company. Before new temps are sent out on an assignment, they are evaluated in terms of skills, personality, attitude and appearance. This screening is accomplished through appropriate skill evaluations and in-person interviews.

The new temp is then evaluated in terms of skill level, work experience and availability. This allows the service to quickly locate the right person to fill a business's needs.

Today's temporary positions are proving to be the best choice for working mothers, empty nesters, moonlighters, retirees—and others who want or need to work when they choose. Temping gives unemployed and displaced individuals a way to make contacts and pay their rent while looking for permanent work. It also provides an opportunity for students and recent college graduates to gain valuable experience while testing the waters at a number of companies.

Some readers will use temping as a stepping stone to permanent positions that would have otherwise been inaccessible. Many others will join the ranks of career temps—those who want or need a more flexible lifestyle that allows more time for family and other outside interests.

"There is a whole new world of opportunity out there," the authors state in concluding this chapter. "Our objectives in the chapters that follow are threefold:

1. To help you assess your particular career and lifestyle needs.
2. To determine how these needs fit with the rapidly expanding opportunities in temporary employment.
3. To map out a personalized temporary employment game plan."

CHAPTER TWO: Is Temping Right for You?
(Please see enclosed sample chapter.)

CHAPTER THREE: Taking Advantage of Expanding Opportunities in Today's and Tomorrow's Temporary Job Market

The authors discuss the dramatic increase in the demand for temps in a wide variety of fields. In evaluating why nearly one hundred percent of all American companies now use temporary help to complement permanent staffs, the authors cite and discuss the following trends:

- Technological advances—particularly those related to computers and the automated office—have led to a shortage of qualified personnel. The ability to use a pc and up-to-date software is becoming a necessity on most jobs. As a result, companies need employees with higher education and skill levels than in the past. Temp services are responding to that need by offering cross-training programs and providing personnel who are skilled in data processing.
- Using temporary help makes it easier for businesses to control screening, hiring and benefits costs, thus enabling them to protect their profit margins.
- A judicious use of temporary help allows companies more flexibility in staffing, and relief from higher fixed personnel costs. By using temps during peak periods and for specific projects, companies are able to operate with a lean permanent staff during normal workload periods.
- Other innovative uses of temps include: hiring back valuable employees lost through mandatory retirement, filling vital jobs during hiring freezes, smoothing the transition of business relocations and filling in for staff who are on vacation or sick leave.

"As we approach the twenty-first century," the authors observe, "we expect the temporary help industry to expand as companies meet the challenges of a shrinking labor market, escalating costs and the overall demand for increased productivity in a global marketplace.

"Temporary help will be an important element in companies' staffing strategies as they seek to cope with fluctuating business cycles and try to get more cost-effective productivity from their operations."

The discussion continues with a look at the different fields and professions that now use the services of temporary personnel. While the largest growth areas for temporary employees are in fields requiring data processing and computerized office skills, there is also an increasing demand for temps in the financial, legal, marketing, education, hospitality, manufacturing and healthcare fields.

The job opportunities in each of these areas are evaluated in terms of current and future demand, necessary skills, experience and earnings requirements. Readers are asked to complete a questionnaire designed to evaluate their skills and financial requirements in terms of the realities of the temporary job market. The chapter concludes with specific suggestions on how to translate the results of this questionnaire into a specific plan of action.

PROPOSAL 9

Heart and Soul

A Psychological and Spiritual Guide to Preventing and Healing Heart Disease

by
Bruno Cortis, M.D.

This project was sold to the Villard Books division of Random House and is set for publication in 1994.

Every editor who saw this proposal had sincere praise for it, but many felt that their health/ spirituality quota was already full and that they would be competing with themselves if they acquired any more such titles.

Market-glut is a familiar problem. In many popular categories, it's almost endemic. But if you're prepared for this reality from the outset, you can pave your own road and bypass the competition. Dedicated agents, editors, and writers want important books published regardless of what the publishers' lists dictate. Further, it's not necessary for every publisher to want your book. In the end, you need only the right publisher and a reasonable deal.

1. This title conjures up dramatic images similar to a soulful blues melody, and it has everything to do with what the proposal is about. The subtitle is scientific and provides a clear direction for the patients.

Overview

2. A powerful lead para-
graph immediately dis-
tinguishes this book pro-
posal from the many
competitive books and
draws attention to "new
research." Anything
that's potentially cutting
edge will catch the eye of
a prospective publisher.

3. This paragraph con-
tains the central thesis
and could have been
used as the first para-
graph of the proposal. It
also contains a clever
comparison to a highly
successful book, while
indicating how the
author's book will merit
the same type of atten-
tion.

4. It's wise to bring the
author's credentials into
the overview. A com-
parison made with Dr.
Siegel will immediately
raise questions as to
whether this author has
similar potential. The
author anticipates this
editorial reasoning and
makes some strong
statements.

5. This is an exceptional
overview—especially
where it defines the
three patient types. It
shows a highly focused
and well thought-out
plan. Although writing
such a good proposal
took effort, there's no
struggle for the editor
to understand exactly
what's being proposed
and what the book will
be about.

Heart disease is the number-one killer of Americans over the age of 2
40. The very words can sound like a death sentence. Our heart, the
most intimate part of our body, is under siege. Until now, most
experts have advised victims of the disease, as well as those who would
avoid it, to change avoidable risk factors, like smoking, and begin a
spartan regimen of diet and exercise. But new research shows that risk
factors and lifestyle are only part of the answer. In fact, it is becoming
clear that for many patients, emotional, psychological, and even spiritual factors are at least as important, both in preventing disease and
in healing an already damaged heart.

Like *Love, Medicine, and Miracles* by Bernie Siegel, which showed 3
cancer patients how to take charge of their own disease and life, *Heart
and Soul* will show potential and actual heart patients how to use inner
resources to form a healthy relationship with their heart, actually
healing circulatory disorders and preventing further damage.

The author, Bruno Cortis, M.D., is a renowned cardiologist whose 4
experience with hundreds of "exceptional heart patients" has taught
him that there is much more to medicine than operations and pills.

Dr. Cortis identifies three types of heart patients:

- Passive Patients, who are unwilling or unable to take respon- 5
  sibility for their condition. Instead, these patients blame outside forces, withdraw from social contacts, and bewail their
  fate. They may become deeply depressed, and tend to die
  very soon.
- Obedient Consumers, who are the "A" students of modern
  medicine. Following doctors' orders to the letter, these
  patients behave exactly as they are "supposed to," placing
  their fates in the hands of the experts. These patients tend to
  die exactly when medicine predicts they will.
- Exceptional Heart Patients, who regard a diagnosis of heart
  disease as a challenge. Although they may have realistic fears
  for the future, these patients take full responsibility for their
  situation and actively contribute to their own recovery. While
  they may or may not follow doctors' orders, these patients
  tend to choose the therapy or combination of therapies that is
  best for them. They often live far beyond medical predictions.

It is Dr. Cortis' aim in this book to show readers how to become
exceptional heart patients, empowering them to take responsibility
for their own health and well-being.

Although Dr. Cortis acknowledges the importance of exercise, stress management, and proper nutrition—the standard staples of cardiac treatment—he stresses that there is an even deeper level of human experience that is necessary in order to produce wellness. Unlike other books on heart disease, *Heart and Soul* does not prescribe the same strict diet and exercise program for everyone. Instead it takes a flexible approach, urging readers to create their own unique health plan by employing psychological and spiritual practices in combination with a variety of more traditional diet and exercise regimens.

While seemingly revolutionary, Dr. Cortis' message is simple: you can do much more for the health of your heart than you think you can. This is true whether you have no symptoms or risk factors whatsoever, if you have some symptoms or risk factors, or if you actually already have heart disease.

Market Analysis

6 *Heart and Soul* could not be more timely. Of the 1 1/2 million heart attacks suffered by Americans each year, nearly half occur between the ages of 40 and 65. Three fifths of these heart attacks are fatal. While these precise statistics may not be familiar to the millions of baby boomers now entering middle age, the national obsession with oat bran, low-fat foods, and exercising for health shows that the members of the boomer generation are becoming increasingly aware of their own mortality.

7 This awareness of growing older, coupled with a widespread loss of faith in doctors and fear of overtechnologized medicine, combine to produce a market that is ready for a book emphasizing the spiritual component in healing, especially in reference to heart disease.

8 Most existing books on the market approach the subject from the physician's point of view, urging readers to follow doctor's orders to attain a healthy heart. There is very little emphasis in these books on the patient's own responsibility for wellness or the inner changes that must be made for the prescribed regimens to work. Among the best known recent books are:

9 *Healing Your Heart*, by Herman Hellerstein, M.D., and Paul Perry (Simon and Schuster, 1990). Although this book, like most of the others, advocates proper nutrition, exercise, cessation of smoking and stress reduction as the road to a healthy heart, it fails to provide the motivation necessary to attain such changes in the reader's lifestyle. Without changes in thinking and behavior, readers of this and similar books will find it difficult, if not impossible, to follow the strict diet and exercise program recommended.

6. A good use of facts, trends, and the public's receptivity to what some would characterize as an unorthodox treatment approach.

7. This section is termed the "market analysis," which differs from the marketing section you see in most proposals. Instead of telling the publisher how to sell the book, the writing collaborator shows special insight into the target audience. This type of in-depth analysis of the potential reader can be very persuasive.

8. It's sometimes helpful to identify this portion of the proposal under a separate "competition" heading.

9. The analysis of the competition highlights the most relevant books on the market without listing each one directly. You might want to use this approach if there are too many similar books in your particular subject area. Notice, though, that the writer confronts the heaviest competition directly by finding specific distinguishing factors that support the strength of his proposed project.

In *Heart Talk: Preventing and Coping with Silent and Painful Heart Disease* (Harcourt Brace Jovanovich, 1987), Dr. Peter F. Cohn and Dr. Joan K. Cohn address the dangers of "silent" (symptomless) heart disease. While informative, the book emphasizes only one manifestation of heart disease, and does not empower readers with the motivational tools needed to combat that disease.

The Trusting Heart, by Redford Williams, M.D. (Times Books, 1989), demonstrates how hostility and anger can lead to heart disease while trust and forgiveness can contribute to wellness. While these are important points, the holistic treatment of heart disease must encompass other approaches as well. The author also fails to provide sufficient motivation for behavioral changes in the readers.

The best book on preventing and curing heart disease is *Dr. Dean Ornish's Program for Reversing Heart Disease* (Random House, 1990). This highly successful book prescribes a very strict diet and exercise program for actually reversing certain types of coronary artery disease. This still-controversial approach is by far the best on the market; unfortunately, the material is presented in a dense, academic style not easily accessible to the lay reader. It also focuses on Dr. Ornish's program as the "only way to manage heart disease, excluding other, more synergistic methods.

10. The author convincingly demonstrates the uniqueness of this particular project—especially important when compared with the strong list of competitors.

Approach

Heart and Soul will be a 60-70,000-word book targeted to health-conscious members of the baby boom generation. Unlike other books on heart disease, it will focus on the "facts of the connection between the mind and the body as it relates to heart disease, showing readers how to use that connection to heal the heart. The book will be written in an informal but authoritative style, in Dr. Cortis' voice. It will begin with a discussion of heart disease and show how traditional medicine fails to prevent or cure it. Subsequent chapters will deal with the mind-body connection, and the role in healing of social support systems, self-esteem, and faith. In order to help readers reduce stress in their lives, Dr. Cortis shows how they can create their own "daily practice" that combines exercise, relaxation, meditation, and use of positive imagery. Throughout the book, he will present anecdotes that demonstrate how other Exceptional Heart Patients have overcome their disease and gone on to lead healthy and productive lives.

In addition to a thorough discussion of the causes and outcomes of coronary artery disease, the book will include tests and checklists that readers may use to gauge their progress, and exercises, ranging from the cerebral to the physical, that strengthen and help heal the heart. At the end of each chapter readers will be introduced to an essential "Heartskill" that will enable them to put the advice of the chapter into immediate practice.

11   Through example and encouragement *Heart and Soul* will offer readers a variety of strategies for coping with heart disease, to be taken at once or used in combination. Above all an accessible, practical book, *Heart and Soul* will present readers with a workable program for controlling their own heart disease and forming a healthy relationship with their hearts.

The Authors

12 Bruno Cortis, M.D., is an internationally trained cardiologist with more than 30 years' experience in research and practice. A pioneer of cardiovascular applications of lasers and angioscopy, a Diplomate of the American Board of Cardiology, contributor of more than 70 published professional papers, Dr. Cortis has long advocated the need for new dimensions of awareness in health and the healing arts. As a practicing physician and researcher, his open acknowledgment of individual spirituality as the core of health puts him on the cutting edge of those in traditional medicine who are beginning to create the medical arts practices of the future.

13   Dr. Cortis has been a speaker at conferences in South America, Japan, and Australia, as well as in Europe and the United States. His firm, Mind Your Health, is dedicated to the prevention of heart attack through the development of human potential. Dr. Cortis is the cofounder of the Exceptional Heart Patients program. The successful changes he has made in his own medical practice prove he is a man not only of vision and deeds, but an author whose beliefs spring from the truths of daily living.

14   Kathryn Lance is the author of more than 30 books of nonfiction and fiction (see attached publications list for details). Her first book, *Running for Health and Beauty* (1976), the first mass market book on running for women, sold half a million copies. *The Setpoint Diet* (1985), ghosted for Dr. Gilbert A. Leveille, reached the New York *Times* best-seller list for several weeks. Ms. Lance has written widely on fitness, health, diet, and medicine.

11. This is a clear summary statement of the book.

12. A very good description of the author. The writing collaborator establishes Dr. Cortis as both an expert in his field and a compelling personality. All of this material is relevant to the book's success.

13. A formal vitae follows. It's best to lead with a journalistic-style biography and follow with a complete and formal resume—assuming, as in this case, the author's professional credentials are inseparable from the book.

14. Although she wasn't mentioned on the title page, Lance is the collaborator. Her bio sketch is strong in its simplicity. Her writing credits are voluminous, but she doesn't use up space here with a comprehensive listing. Instead she showcases only credits relevant to the success of this particular project. Comprehensive author resumes were also attached to the proposal package as addendums.

15. As we stated in other proposal critiques, a separate table of contents would have been useful.

16. This exceptional outline goes beyond the often lazy and stingy telegraph approach many writers use, often to their own detriment. Here each abstract reads like a miniature sample chapter unto itself. It proves that the writers as a team have a genuine command of their subject, a well-organized agenda, and superior skills for writing about it. Some writers are reluctant to do this much work on speculation. However, if you believe in your project's viability, and you want to maximize acquisition interest and the ultimate advance, you'll be wise to give the proposal everything you've got.

17. In this interesting technique for a chapter abstract, the writer organizes the structure as a listing of chapter topics and elaborates with a sample of the substance and writing approach that will be incorporated into the book. The editor will come away with a good sense of the quality of the chapter and the depth of its coverage.

Heart and Soul
by Bruno Cortis, M.D.

Chapter Outline

Table of Contents   *15*

Introduction: Beating the Odds: Exceptional Heart Patients.
See sample chapter.

Chapter One. You and Your Heart.   *16*

Traditional medicine doesn't and can't "cure" heart disease. The recurrence rate of arterial blockage after angioplasty is 25–35%, while a bypass operation only *bypasses* the problem, but does not cure it. The author proposes a new way of looking at heart disease, one in which *17* patients become responsible for the care and well-being of their hearts, in partnership with their physicians. Following a brief, understandable discussion of the physiology of heart disease and heart attack, further topics covered in this chapter include:

Heart disease as a message from your body. Many of us go through life *18* neglecting our bodies' signals, ignoring symptoms until a crisis occurs. But the body talks to us and it is up to us to listen and try to understand the message. The heart bears the load of all our physical activity as well as our mental activity. Stress can affect the heart as well as any other body system. This section explores the warning signs of heart disease as "messages" we may receive from our hearts, what these messages may mean, and what we can do in response to these messages.

Why medical tests and treatments are not enough. You, the patient, are ultimately responsible for your own health. Placing all faith in a doctor is a way of abdicating that responsibility. The physician is not a healer; rather, he or she sets the stage for the patient's body to heal itself. Disease is actually a manifestation of an imbalance within the body. Medical procedures can help temporarily, but the real solution lies in the patient's becoming aware of his own responsibility for health. This may involve changing diet, stopping smoking, learning to control the inner life.

Getting the best (while avoiding the worst) of modern medicine. In the author's view, the most important aspect of medicine is not the medication but the patient/physician relationship. Unfortunately, this relationship is often cold, superficial, professional. The patient goes into the medical pipeline, endures a number of tests, then comes out the other end with a diagnosis which is like a flag he has to carry for life. This view of disease ignores the patient as the *main* component of the healing process. Readers are advised to work with their doctors to learn their own blood pressure, blood sugar, cholesterol level, and what these numbers mean. They are further advised how to enlist a team of support people to increase their own knowledge of the disease and learn to discover the self-healing mechanisms within.

How to assess your doctor. Ten questions a patient needs to ask in order to assure the best patient-doctor relationship.

Taking charge of your own medical care. Rather than being passive patients, readers are urged to directly confront their illness and the reasons for it, asking themselves: how can I find a cause at the deepest level? What have I learned from this disease? What is good about it? What have I learned about myself? Exceptional heart patients don't allow themselves to be overwhelmed by the disease; rather, they realize that it is most likely a temporary problem, most of the time self-limited, and that they have a power within to overcome it.

Seven keys to a healthy heart. Whether presently healthy or already ill of heart disease there is a great deal readers can do to improve and maintain the health of their hearts. The most important component of such a plan is to have a commitment to a healthy heart. The author offers the following seven keys to a healthy heart: respect your body; take time to relax every day; accept, respect, and appreciate yourself; share your deepest feelings; establish life goals; nourish your spiritual self; love yourself and others unconditionally. Each of these aspects of heart care will be examined in detail in later chapters.

Heartskill #1: *Learning to take your own pulse.* The pulse is a wave of blood sent through the arteries each time the heart contracts; pulse rate therefore provides important information about cardiac function. The easiest place to measure the pulse is the wrist: place your index and middle finger over the underside of the opposite wrist. Press gently and firmly until you locate your pulse. Don't use your thumb to feel the pulse, because the thumb has a pulse of its own. Count the number of pulse beats in fifteen seconds, then multiply that by four for your heart rate.

This exercise will include charts so that readers can track and learn their own normal pulse range for resting and exercising, and be alerted to irregularities and changes that may require medical attention.

18. Although the abstracts are directed to the editor who reviews the proposal, the writer incorporates the voice to be used in the book by speaking directly to the reader. An effective way to get her writing style into the chapter-by-chapter outline.

19. This shows that specific and practical information will be included in the book—which is generally important for nonfiction. Editors look for these "program aspects" because they can be used in promotional settings such as electronic media, as well as in catchy serial-rights selections targeted toward magazines.

Chapter Two. Your Mind and Your Heart.

This chapter begins to explore the connection between mind and body as it relates to heart disease. Early in the chapter readers will meet three Exceptional Heart Patients who overcame crushing diagnoses. These include Van, who overcame a heart attack (at age 48), two open heart surgeries, and "terminal" lung cancer. Through visu- [20] alization techniques given him by the author, Van has fully recovered and is living a healthy and satisfying life. Goran, who had a family history of cardiomyopathy, drew on the support and love of his family to survive a heart transplant and has since gone on to win several championships in an Olympics contest for transplant patients. Elaine, who overcame both childhood cancer and severe heart disease, is, at the age of 24, happily married and a mother. The techniques used by these Exceptional Heart Patients will be discussed in the context of the mind-body connection.

How your doctor views heart disease: risk factors v. symptoms. Traditional medicine views the risk factors for heart disease (smoking, high blood cholesterol, high blood pressure, diabetes, obesity, sedentary lifestyle, family history of heart disease, use of oral contraceptives) as indicators of the likelihood of developing illness. In contrast, the author presents these risk factors as *symptoms* of an underlying disease, and discusses ways to change them. Smoking, for example, is not the root of the problem, which is, rather, fear, tension, and stress. Smoking is just an outlet that the patient uses to get rid of these basic elements which he or she believes are uncontrollable. Likewise high cholesterol, which is viewed by the medical establishment as largely caused by poor diet, is also affected by stress. (In a study of rabbits on a high-cholesterol diet, narrowing of arteries was less in rabbits that were petted, even if the diet remained unhealthful.) Other elements besides the traditional "risk factors," such as hostility, have been shown to lead to high rates of heart disease.

A mind/body model of heart disease. It is not uncommon to hear stories like this: they were a very happy couple, married 52 years. Then, suddenly, the wife developed breast cancer and died. The husband, who had no previous symptoms of heart disease, had a heart attack and died two months later. All too often there is a very close relationship between a traumatic event and serious illness. Likewise, patients may often become depressed and literally will themselves to die. The other side of the coin is the innumerable patients who use a variety of techniques to enlist the mind-body connection in helping to overcome and even cure serious illnesses, including heart disease.

20. The authors do not save the good stuff for the book. If you have interesting case studies or anecdotes, include them in your abstract. The more stimulating material you can include, the more you will intrigue your potential editor.

Rethinking your negative beliefs about heart disease. The first step in using the mind to help to heal the body is to rethink negative beliefs about heart disease. Modern studies have shown that stress plays a most important role in the creation of heart disease, influencing all of the "risk factors." Heart disease is actually a disease of self, caused by self, and is made worse by the belief that we are its "victims." Another negative and incorrect belief is that the possibilities for recovery are limited. The author asserts that these beliefs are untrue, and that for patients willing to learn from the experience, heart disease can be a path to recovery, self-improvement, and growth.

The healing personality: tapping into your body's healing powers. Although the notion of a "healing personality" may sound contradictory, the power of healing is awareness, which can be achieved by anyone. The author describes his own discovery of spirituality in medicine and the realization that ultimately the origin of disease is in the mind. This is why treating disease with medicine and surgery alone does not heal: because these methods ignore the natural healing powers of the body/mind. How does one develop a "healing personality"? The starting point is awareness of the spiritual power within. As the author states, in order to become healthy, one must become spiritual.

Writing your own script for a healthy heart. Before writing any script, one must set the stage, and in this case readers are urged to see a cardiologist or physician and have a thorough checkup. This checkup will evaluate the presence or absence of the "risk factors," and assess the health of other body organs as well. Once the scene is set, it is time to add in the other elements of a healthy heart, all of which will be explored in detail in the coming chapters.

Making a contract with your heart. We see obstacles only when we lose sight of our goals. How to make out (either mentally or on paper) a contract with one's heart that promises to take care of the heart. Each individual reader's contract will be somewhat different; for example, someone who is overweight might include in the contract the desire that in six months she would weigh so much. The point is to set realistic, achievable goals. Guidelines are provided for breaking larger goals down into small, easily achievable, steps. Creating goals for the future makes them a part of the present in the sense that it is today that we start pursuing them.

What to say when you talk to yourself. In the view of the author, the greatest source of stress in life is negative conversations we have with ourselves. These "conversations," which go on all the time without our even being aware of them, often include such negative suggestions as "When are you going to learn?" "Oh, no, you stupid idiot, you did it again!" When we put ourselves down we reinforce feelings of unworthiness and inadequacy, which leads to stress and illness. Guidelines are given for replacing such negative self-conversation with more positive self-talk, including messages of love and healing.

Heartskill #2: *Sending healing energy to your heart.* In this exercise, [21] readers learn a simple meditation technique that will help them get in touch with their natural healing powers and begin to heal their hearts.

21. The chapter abstract in the proposal continued on to the end, but the first two chapters show you why this proposal was effective.

PROPOSAL 10

Talk Your Way to the Top
Communication Secrets of the CEOs

by
Stephen R. Maloney

This proposal was sold to Prentice Hall.

Several publishers saw this proposal and almost all were very positive about its merits, but again the main obstacle was that the category (communication) is saturated. This is true for many nonfiction categories, but good and original material can smash through the logjam and succeed—which is what happened here.

This proposal isn't exceptionally strong until you reach the outline. The book then comes alive with a well-organized synopsis that gives the flavor of what's to come.

Overview

"An executive does nothing more important than speak." (Jere Stead, [1] Chief Executive Officer, Square D, Inc.)

I direct my manuscript to the great mass of managers, would-be managers, and professionals who make presentations, from informal one-on-one sessions with the boss to formal one-on-a-thousand speeches. I show how the same principles work for all presentations.

I explain how speakers can analyze their strengths and weaknesses—and challenge them to do so. I emphasize that successful presentations spring from the rigorous application of simple principles.

Why should a well-written book on my subject sell briskly? [2] **Because communication is the foundation of all the skills needed by modern managers:** providing leadership; selecting and developing personnel; making investment recommendations; managing technology; and communicating with important audiences inside and outside a company.

I provide a systematic approach to developing better communication habits. In clear, simple prose, I tell people how to analyze their speech habits; I show how they can use this analysis to make themselves more persuasive and effective communicators.

Overall, I unlock the mystery underlying such subjects as: how to [3] move an audience to action; how to avoid the hazards connected with visual aids; how to use humor without laying eggs; and how to deal with the special communication challenges facing women.

I don't just give advice; instead, I share with readers the techniques that business leaders use to communicate effectively. Because I've worked on presentations with 19 heads of Fortune 500 companies, I write from an insider's perspective. I show that the principles I'm advocating have worked for America's most successful executives.

In recent years, books by Lee Iacocca, John Scully, Mark McCormick, Robert Townshend, and other executives have been heavy sellers. I hope to draw on the strong public interest in what CEOs are really like and how they got to the top.

In my concluding chapter, I point out that successful communi- [4] cators generally have successful lives. As we learn how to make good presentations, we should gain confidence in our abilities and control over our lives. It sounds somewhat like positive thinking. It's really about **positive doing**—positive communicating. That skill might not move mountains, it *will* move audiences.

---

1. The opening statements are perfectly clear and sound. The author sets the table with the expectation that he can and will teach valuable presentation skills. However, he overuses the pronoun "I" and its possessive form "my." This can be a detriment with some editors. It's easy to change self-references to a more neutral tone, for example, changing "I direct my manuscript . . ." to "This manuscript will appeal to the great mass . . ."

2. This paragraph is a bit misplaced. The argument would be better addressed in the marketing section. Also, the reference to "my subject" should be changed to "this subject."

3. The author provides credible reasons why this book should exist.

4. This provocative paragraph states a reasonable contention that effective communicators lead better lives, and the author promises to support the theory.

Market Analysis

5 My commercial goals? To get people to manage to spend a lot more than one minute with a book whose underlying theme is: "Address for Success." My market niche should be a large one: the millions of current and prospective business managers and professionals faced with making presentations. I want to show them how to make presentations without anxiety and to influence and impress their bosses. Professionally printed, promoted, and marketed, this book can be a successful seller.

The best in-print books on making and writing presentations are either reference books or academic efforts. Unlike my manuscript, they're not aimed at the mass market of status-conscious business people obsessed with getting ahead.

The best reference book is Brent Filson's *Executive Speeches* (Williamstown Publishing Company, 1990, $49.95). The top academic effort is Kathryn Hall Jamieson's *Eloquence in an Electronic Age* (Oxford University Press, 1988, $24.95). Filson (who quotes me extensively) developed his fine book from interviews with CEOs. It's an excellent book full of good advice, and it has sold well given its price tag, which nevertheless reflects its target market: libraries and executives with library-like bookshelves. Jamieson's book is a superb historical study of political speechmakers, but it's aimed at scholars.

Peggy Noonan wrote a good seller about speechwriting and speechmaking in the Reagan White House: *What I Saw at the Revolution: A Political Life in the Reagan Era* (Random House, 1990, $19.95). There is some superb commentary about speechwriting, but her book is about "talking at the top," not about how to talk your way there.

6 There are more than 120 books in print about public speaking. Most of them merit their relatively low prices and short shelf-lives. They fall into two categories: (1) limited-interest paperbacks giving "cookbook" hints to people faced with addressing the local garden society or Rotary Club and (2) textbooks.

On the garden society/Rotary Club list, no one has yet outdone Dale Carnegie's book, first published in 1926 as *Public Speaking and Influencing Men in Business*. The best recent example of a general-interest book about public speaking is Dorothy Leeds's *Powerspeak* (Prentice Hall, 1988, $17.95). The sales curve for this book is heading toward ground zero. In addition, unlike my manuscript, it doesn't have my CEO hook.

5. It's evident that a lively market exists for this information and that the author has a good plan for this book. This is a strong marketing section.

6. The author sneaks in the statement that there are some 120 titles on that subject, but summarily dismisses them as being of low quality. This weak statement of competition gives agents and editors no supporting evidence.

Overall, my book should appeal to individuals looking for a competitive edge in a tough job marketplace. It may be lonely at the top, but there are a lot of people who want to scale the mountain. They're the ones who will buy my book.

Special Marketing Opportunities

7. This is a good addition. The author is not engaging in wishful thinking; these programs actually exist. Besides citing the Aetna program, the author should have listed other such programs.

My manuscript should fit well into the growing executive-education [7] market, where little good material on presentations exists. For example, Aetna (my employer) sends more than 2,000 managers and professionals per year through its courses in communications. My book is a natural buy for this company's educational programs and for other programs like it.

The book also should be marketed to the companies (more than 30, with more than 500,000 employees) mentioned in the book. Finally, because the book is such a natural for upwardly mobile managers, the publisher should offer it to book clubs, including BOMC, Fortune, and the Executive Program.

My Approach

My approach is to demystify presentation making. The book will give a simple, clear, logical approach to analyzing and improving the reader's ability to speak before one or more people.

The manuscript will be a cover-to-cover read on a coast-to-coast flight. Also, specific chapters, such as the two on how to write a speech for the boss, allow for selective reading.

As the detailed outline indicates, this project is well along in conception and organization. The book should be about 35,000 words, approximately seven times as long as the chapter outline. I will complete it within six months of signing a contract and receiving an advance that would free me to work on it full time.

Credentials

8. It's always beneficial when an author can open with a strong statement like this—as long as it's then supported.

Stephen R. Maloney is one of the most successful and highly regarded [8] corporate speechwriters in the world. He has written for 19 chief executive officers (including Lee Iacocca) at Fortune 500 corporations and two heads of major trade associations. He has directed executive communications at Phillips Petroleum, USX, Gulf Oil, Allegheny International, and Aetna, where he heads the speechwriting and financial communications department. He supervised executive and share-holder communications at Gulf during T. Boone Pickens' hostile take-over attempt in 1983/1984.

9   Maloney has either ghosted or written under his own name articles for *Fortune, Newsweek,* the *American Spectator, National Review,* the *Wall Street Journal,* and the *New York Times.* He has lectured on speech-writing and has written on the subject for the *Public Relations Journal* and *Speechwriter's Newsletter,* where he wrote a humor and lifestyle column for two years.

9. There's no fat in this author presentation section; these credentials show muscle.

Prior to working in business, Maloney taught literature and writing courses at the College of William and Mary and the University of Georgia, where he also was assistant editor of the *Georgia Review.*

10   Maloney received a Ph.D. in English and American Literature from the University of Rochester, where he was a New York State Regents Fellow. He was one of the first individuals in the nation to achieve a perfect score (850) on the verbal section of the Graduate Record Exam.

10. Although not necessarily relevant, his perfect score on the GRE is pretty impressive.

Chapter Outline:

Talk Your Way to the Top: Communication Secrets of the CEOs

Foreword: We Are What We Say . . . and How We Say It

Chapter 1: The CEOs: Communications and the Passion for Self-Improvement

Chapter 2: Take Your Presentation "I.Q."

Chapter 3: Surefire Techniques for Presentation Success

Chapter 4: Express Your Convictions!

Chapter 5: The Closer: Start with Your Conclusion

Chapter 6: Organization Flows from Intentions

Chapter 7: Put It (Your Presentation) on Paper (or on Tape)

Chapter 8: Practice Makes (Almost) Perfect

Chapter 9: Graphics? Only When They're Truly *Graphic*

Chapter 10: Don't Tell Jokes—Share Experience

Chapter 11: Make the Q & A More A Than Q

Chapter 12: Write a Speech for The Boss? Yes You Can!

Chapter 13: Remember, a Speech Is *Not* an Essay

Chapter 14: Fear? Strike It Out of Your Vocabulary

Chapter 15: Women: Special Challenges, Special Opportunities

Chapter 16: Effective Communication: The Art of Remaking Yourself

Note: In the chapter outline, the text in regular format represents a preliminary version of the writing that will appear in the manuscript; the text in boxes suggests the direction of the additional material that will appear in each chapter. The completed manuscript will be approximately 35,000 words.

Foreword: We Are What We Say . . . and How We Say It

Mary Richards (Mary Tyler Moore, having been asked to direct her [11] first news show): "But, Mr. Grant, I have trouble asserting myself."

Grant (Edward Asner, reading a programming schedule): "Uhh . . . ."
Richards: "People just won't *listen* to me."
Grant (looking up): "Whadya say?"

Words—not numbers—are the true currency of business, and [12] **government, and our social lives.** Business people, teachers, politicians, clerics: all of them rise or fall on their ability to use the language. Their communications success reinforces their conviction, self-assurance, and leadership.

In the past 15 years, I've worked on major speeches and other presentations with more than 50 senior executives at Fortune 500 companies. Many times, I've "put words in their mouths." More often, these high-achieving men and women have put ideas in my head about the secrets of successful communication.

The central secret I've learned is this: **we are what we say . . . and how we say it**. We are *Homo verbus*, creatures of words. We use them, but they define us — our social status and economic potential.

The business chief executive officers and other top executives have taught me two related secrets:

- First, great speakers are made, not born; that is, **we can gain control over what we say and how we say it**.
- Second, **as we improve our ability to communicate, we enhance people's impressions of us**.

The principles in this book are for individuals who have to sell products, proposals, principles—or themselves. They're for men and women who want to emulate the decisiveness and the persuasiveness of those occupying seats of power. The same communication secrets that work in a conversation will work in a formal address.

---

11. This dialog is effective. It's disarming and creates a visual of the problem.

12. An excellent example of what an outline should be: It successfully integrates style with substance while not overwhelming with detail. The tone is just right for this type of book, and the outline fulfills what the proposal promises.

The principles in this book will unlock potential you never knew you had. Knowledge is the enemy of fear, and **when you use the information in this book, you'll never again fear making presentations**.

The communication secrets of the CEOs are nothing more than prescriptions you can learn and use. In so doing, you will experience the exhilarating personal growth that comes from identifying your communication failings and transforming them into strengths.

Chapter 1: The CEOs: Their Passion for Self-Improvement

You can't improve your communications skills if you accept the defeatist notion that "I am what I am." **CEOs get into the executive suite the same way that a John F. Kennedy became a great communicator/President: through a tenacious commitment to self-improvement**. We know Kennedy as one of our finest political orators. Yet early in his presidency, Kennedy was so nervous about speaking in public that his left hand would shake uncontrollably.

That fact didn't stop him from making memorable speeches and presiding at witty, informative press conferences. As for his shaky left hand, he put it in his pocket. With his firm right hand, he gestured with "vigah."

After Kennedy's death, one of his friends and associates wrote a book called *Johnny, We Hardly Knew Ya*. But we did "know" him, more through his speeches and news conferences than through his deeds. Kennedy, like his hero Churchill, used words to forge his place in history.

Unlike Kennedy and Churchill, most senior business executives are not born to wealth and power. Bill Martin of Phillips Petroleum is the son of a Dust-Bowl-era grain warehouseman in Oklahoma; Martin's successor, Bill Douce, is the offspring of a rural Kansas pharmacist; Dave Roderick of USX is the son of a postman; Roderick's executive colleagues Bill Roesch and Al Hillegas were born in steel towns and worked in Pittsburgh-area steel mills. Ron Compton of Aetna is the son of a South Chicago insurance salesman.

Bill Douce is tougher than a $1.99 steak. He capped off his superb career at Phillips by fighting off a hostile takeover by the legendary T. Boone Pickens, Jr. One of Douce's colleagues from his early days recalls that the future chairman "didn't know anything when he came to Phillips. But he used to carry a notepad everywhere he went, and he'd write down everything he learned."

Aristotle said, "All men desire by nature to know." He could have been referring to the CEOs I've known. Their curiosity is boundless;

their motto could be: "Do it better the next time." Whatever limitations the accident of birth imposes on them, they seek to overcome.

The best of the CEOs are their own toughest critics. They also seek out constructive criticism from others. An example: early in my career, I worked on a speech for Phillips Petroleum CEO Bill Martin. After he delivered it, we were flying back to Oklahoma, and he asked for my assessment of his performance.

Awed by this powerful industrialist, a former All-American basketball player who retained his movie-star looks into his 60s, I gushed: "You were terrific, boss."

He frowned and said, "I don't need that."

His point was that sycophantic praise would not help him. He wanted specific information about what he'd done right and, even more, where he'd fallen short. With that knowledge, he could do a better job next time.

13. These boxes were in the original proposal. It's not a technique we've encountered before or since, nor is it one we urge you to adopt. But if they are handled well and enhance rather than distract, there's no reason to oppose such special effects. Like sidebars in a lengthy article, these boxes open windows into deeper insights and make overall comprehension easier.

13

This chapter will illustrate the CEO's obsession with feedback, and with improving their presentation delivery; CEOs are not passive acceptors of their fate. Engineers, economists, and accountants by training, they learn to communicate as they rise in organizations. They watch videos of their performances (Aetna's Ron Compton says "If you're not good on TV, you're not good."); they solicit objective comments on their presentations; they work on their weaknesses. They know good communication is the foundation of leadership. Like their presentations themselves, these leaders are relentless. This is the secret of their overall success.

Chapter 2: Take Your Presentation "I.Q."
The first step in communicating better is to become your own best critic.

The next time you participate in a meeting or give a presentation, capture it on videotape or audiotape. Then, listen to yourself with cold objectivity. Rate yourself on a scale of 1 to 10, with speakers like Churchill, Kennedy, and Roosevelt weighing in around 9-10. If we're honest, most of us put ourselves at 5 or below.

What keeps us out of the category of silver-tongued orators? We mumble and stumble. We punctuate our sentences with more "ahs" than a throat doctor's patients. We inject anxious "you knows" in our utterances. We mumble in monotones. We deliver our statements without punch or decisiveness. We fall into illogic. We digress. Demosthenes we're not.

Speech is a window to the mind and the emotions. If we're confused, anxious, or just plain bashful, our statements will reflect those conditions.

Take the following example. It's drawn from a statement by Billy Sullivan, then the general manager of the New England Patriots, at the time the worst team in professional football. A reporter asked Sullivan if he was about to be fired. Sullivan replied: "I think . . . ah . . . that I . . . ah . . . have things . . . ah . . . to add . . . ah . . . to this . . . ah . . . organization."

He sounded like a man about to be fired, and he "resigned" shortly afterward.

Contrast Sullivan's indecisiveness with the statement of another New England sportsman, Tom Heinsohn, formerly a Boston Celtics star and later a coach and announcer. When asked how one should play in a game against an inferior opponent, Heinsohn said: "Take 'em seriously. Play hard early. Keep your foot on their throat."

Sullivan speaks without forethought, direction, or conviction. In Heinsohn's case, his words have the force of a heavyweight champion's right hook. His sentences are short, the words mostly monosyllabic, the central image (foot/throat) colorful.

The rest of the chapter outlines a systematic way to analyze one's own verbal skills. That analysis is the cornerstone of improving one's ability to communicate. The chapter provides examples of the extensive use of audiotapes and, especially, videotapes, by successful executives.

Chapter 3: Surefire Techniques for Presentation Success

In preparing any oral statement, remember the five "Ps": great *pre*-sentations result from *preparation, practice, persuasiveness,* and *persistency*.

Spontaneous effusions do not make for great presentations. Many of the executives I've worked with spend 20 hours or more thinking about and helping compose an address that may last 20 minutes. Generally, the more time spent in *preparation,* the more powerful the presentation.

The second factor is *persuasiveness,* the ability to make your case to others.

The third factor is *practice*, the habit of reviewing a presentation until it becomes a part of the speaker.

This chapter discusses George Bush's greatest speech: his acceptance remarks at the 1988 Republican National Convention. A notoriously erratic speaker, Bush rehearsed his speech no less than 13 times. When the audience "read his lips," his favorable rating in the polls skyrocketed.

The fourth element is *persistency*, the willingness to stick to the task of improving one's communications skills. I cite the case of Gulf Executive Vice President Harold Hammer, a notoriously poor presenter who metamorphosed himself into a good one. Hammer improved his communication skills through the force of will. He solicited speech opportunities; he also devoted large amounts of time to self-analysis, rehearsal, and active involvement in the development of presentations. He became one of Gulf's most credible speakers.

In this chapter, I explain how to "polish your uncut diamonds," that is, how to make sentences shine, with concise phrasing and memorable words. I cite examples from the CEOs: Bob Buckley on his rapid rise at GE: "I went up in that company like my last name was Electric." Bill Douce: "We've got to stop bellyaching about government (price controls). We've got to clean up our own house first." Aetna's Ron Compton (on his company's plan to withdraw from unprofitable businesses): "Where it doesn't pay, we won't play." Lee Iacocca: "In foreign trade, we need a level playing field."

Book Proposal Terms

About the Author(s) section (see **author biography**)

abstract In a book proposal, a concise rundown of a chapter (or some-times a section) of the proposed book. It conveys the essentials in a way that shows what you can write—without your having to write it all. Chapter abstracts may be viewed as miniature chapters fine-tuned to persuade as well as to answer likely editorial questions. An abstract (along with a separate table of contents) is a part of the book's out-line, and often features elements of the author's intended writing style, anecdotes, and lists of prospective interviewees.

author background (see **author biography**)

author biography The author background or About the Author(s) section of a book proposal. It contains any information about the author(s) that may be pertinent to the book project and is typically placed at the end of the main body of the proposal and before the outline. It may be followed by a separate formal resume or complete vita.

buyback A situation in which an author buys copies of the finished book from the publisher—the number of which may be stipulated before-hand. This figure may come into play during negotiations for a book-publishing contract, whereby the author agrees to purchase (at least) a predetermined number of copies for a specified price. This provides the publisher with a guaranteed sales and circulation base, and may allow the publisher to print more copies, thereby lowering manufac-turing costs per copy. Alternately, an author may simply bargain for the right to buy copies at a hefty discount.

competition The competition section of a book proposal should cover books comparable to the one being proposed. Competing books are existing titles—those in print or formerly in print—with contents or subject area similar to that of the proposed work or that address the same basic target market. This section gives a rundown of at least the higher-profile competing works and distinguishes the proposed book in such terms as innovativeness of approach, comprehensiveness, or scope of potential readership base.

extract Basically a sample. In a book proposal, an extract represents the actual contents or style of the book and may be seen in the outline, for instance, as a slice of the fuller version of an anecdote, a chapter opening, or pertinent quotation from an interview source.

hook A catchphrase (or sometimes just a word) that signifies the essence of your product in the marketing arena: your book's public face, which will be displayed to the agent, editor, publisher, and reader. Just as a hook for a piece of popular music may be a portion of the melody, a lyric line, or a brief instrumental riff, the hook for your book proposal is the powerpoint from which your ideas take flight. Finding a hook for your book is the process of distilling its complex ideas and then depicting them in terms equivalent to a television soundbite.

lead An opening statement. Its point is to get attention—be it in a query letter, book proposal, book manuscript, news story, sales brochure, political speech, or press release.

market Marketing is an aspect of book publishing concerned generally with ensuring the distribution of a book so that it will be available for its target audience, or market. Consideration of a book's potential market is addressed in a book proposal's marketing section, sometimes phrased in terms of who will read/need this book.

outline A charting of a book's contents, most often prefaced by a separate table of contents. The outline may take the simple form of chapter headings followed by an abstract or synopsis of that chapter. Often other pertinent elements are included, such as illustrations (or indications thereof), subheadings, and extracts from interviews, anecdotes, or questionnaires.

overview Typically, the first section of a book proposal—immediately following the title page. It conveys the book's primary message, usually leading with the book's hook and maybe a punchy thesis statement, followed by a brief synopsis of the projected contents—and anything else that should be placed up front. In this section, power writing really comes into play.

program A program in a commercial nonfiction book accents the how-to elements of the topic. It provides a progressive (programmatic), often step-by-step goal-directed plan of achievement that is central to the concerns of interested readers.

promotion The promotional aspects of book publishing include advertising schedules and cataloging, as well as such nuances as coordinating distribution and publicity. Successful book proposals often include listings of the author's promotional achievements as well as a selection of original ideas in this section.

publicity In book publishing a part of the promotion and marketing wing that concentrates on bringing the book and/or the author to the attention of the media. It's sometimes said that the difference between promotion and publicity is that publicity is free. That observation may be true in the sense that news coverage is not regularly sold like advertising; but a publicist writes the original press release and sets up the interview contacts for television and radio appearances—and, like everything else, good publicists don't come cheap. Noting in your book proposal that you have retained a publicist (or will do so) can give you a leg up.

query In book publishing, a written communication (usually a letter of introduction, sometimes including ancillary materials such as selected press clips and/or author resume) geared to entice the publisher, editor, or agent to request a look at the author's book proposal package—or in fiction, the completed outline and manuscript.

query letter (see **query**)

sales The actual selling of the completed volumes—to bookstores and ultimately to the reader. Besides the traditional bookstore outlets, many book sales today are accomplished through direct-response techniques such as targeted mailings and telephone 800 numbers, as well as through alternative venues such as specialty stores (that are not primarily bookstores), and back-of-the-room sales kiosks set up in tandem with workshops, symposiums, conferences, and conventions. In a book proposal, qualified authors do well to cite specific and pertinent suggestions for fresh sales avenues as well as their experience relevant to the sales arena.

sample chapter Book proposal packages most often include a completed portion of the proposed book—this is typically a sample chapter or chapters. Sample chapters allow an editor to get a feel for the author's writing style.

SASE The ubiquitously requested SASE is a self-addressed stamped envelope the author encloses when corresponding by mail with agents, editors, and publishers—all of whom greatly appreciate this courtesy.

synopsis A summary of the content and intent of something. In a book proposal, a synopsis of the book as a whole is generally a component of the overview, while chapter-by-chapter synopses, also termed chapter abstracts, are presented in the outline section.

SUGGESTED READING

Appelbaum, Judith, *How to Get Happily Published* (Third Edition) (New York: Harper & Row, 1988; NAL, 1989). Beyond the "mere" acceptance of a manuscript, this work provides sensible advice on generating ideas, putting them into words, and maintaining control over the editing, sales, and marketing of one's work.

Appelbaum, Judith, Nancy Evans, and Florence Janovic, *The Sensible Solutions How to Get Happily Published Handbook* (New York: Sensible Solutions, 1981). Provides worksheets and additional information for authors of trade books, designed to be used in conjunction with the above-mentioned title.

The Associated Press, *The Associated Press Stylebook and Libel Manual* (Reading, MA: Addison-Wesley, 1987). This easy-to-use, dictionary-format guide is an excellent quick-reference to contemporary journalistic and mainstream word usage. It's far from comprehensive, but answers most frequently encountered writing questions. Treatment of issues pertaining to libel is a must-read for investigative and opinionative writing.

The Association of American University Presses Directory (New York: AAUP, published annually). Gives a detailed description of each AAUP member press with a summary of its publishing program, names and responsibilities of key staff, and requirements for submitting proposals and manuscripts.

Balkin, Richard, *How to Understand and Negotiate a Book Contract or Magazine Agreement* (Cincinnati: Writer's Digest Books, 1985). Essential reading for every writer who stands to make a sale.

Bernard, Andre, editor, *Rotten Rejections* (Wainscott, NY: Pushcart Press, 1990). A humorous and harrowing collection of literary demurrals, including such rejects as William Faulkner, Gustave Flaubert, James Joyce, and Vladimir Nabokov. Fine inspiration for writers encountering rejection during any phase of their careers.

Bernstein, Theodore, *The Careful Writer: A Modern Guide to English Usage* (New York: Atheneum, 1965). An incomparable, lively, accurate, and exquisitely articulate classic in its field. Mainstream and mass-market writers may view it as too high-toned a tome to grace their shelves, but this work nevertheless addresses their needs accessibly with observations they might well heed.

Bernstein, Theodore, *Miss Thistlebottom's Hobgoblins: The Careful Writer's Guide to the Taboos, Bugbears, and Outmoded Rules of English Usage* (New York: Simon & Schuster, 1984). More apt insights from the author of the above-listed work.

Boston, Bruce O., editor, *Stet! Tricks of the Trade for Writers and Editors* (Alexandria, VA: Editorial Experts, 1986). A supple, interactive collection of articles that sets the writer inside the heads of editors and publishers.

Boswell, John, *The Awful Truth About Publishing: Why They Always Reject Your Manuscript . . . And What You Can Do About It* (New York: Warner Books, 1986). A view from the other side—that is, from inside the large publishing house.

Bunnin, Brad, and Peter Beren, *Author Law and Strategies: A Personal Guide for the Working Writer* (Berkeley: Nolo Press, 1984). The ins and outs of publishing laws, published by specialists in do-it-yourself legal guides.

Burgett, Gordon, *The Writer's Guide to Query Letters and Cover Letters* (Rocklin, CA: Prima, 1992). Sound and pointed advice from an expert perspective on how to utilize the query and cover letter to sell your writing.

The Chicago Manual of Style (Chicago: University of Chicago Press, 1982). In matters of editorial style—punctuation, spelling, capitalization, issues of usage—this book provides traditional, conservative, justifiable guidelines. Long considered by many to be the last word on such matters, the *Chicago Manual* is not, however, set up for ease of use as a quick-reference guide; it's not a handbook of grammar per se and doesn't offer writers ready tips for solving day-to-day creative problems. The manual is, rather, a professional reference work for the publishing and editing trade—and in this area it remains the American standard. Many commercial writers and editors characterize the *Manual* as intricate in organization and arcanely indexed relative to their own stylistic concerns.

Curtis, Richard, *Beyond the Bestseller: A Literary Agent Takes You Inside the Book Business* (New York: NAL, 1989; Plume, 1990). Incisive and practical advice for writers from a literary agent who is also an accomplished author.

Curtis, Richard, *How to Be Your Own Literary Agent: The Business of Getting Your Book Published* (Boston: Houghton Mifflin, 1984). Insights and how-to; a personal point of view from one who knows the ropes and shows them to you.

Davidson, Jeffrey P., *Marketing for the Home-Based Business* (Holbrook, MA: Bob Adams, 1991). For entrepreneurs of all stripes (including writers) who are based in their homes. Digs beneath the obvious and uncovers ways to project a high-level image and transform your computer, telephone, and fax into a dynamic marketing staff.

Goldberg, Natalie, *Writing Down the Bones: Freeing the Writer Within* (Boston: Shambhala Publications, 1986). Offers some thoughts and advice on the art of writing. The author is a Zen Buddhist and writing instructor.

Harman, Eleanor, and Ian Montagnes, editors, *The Thesis and the Book* (Toronto: University of Toronto Press, 1976). A selection of articles detailing revision of the scholarly presentation into one with broader appeal. The discussion of the demands of specialist audiences versus those of a wider market is pertinent to the development of general nonfiction projects—especially those involving collaboration between writing professionals and academics.

Herman, Jeff, *Insider's Guide to Book Editors, Publishers, and Literary Agents* (Rocklin, CA: Prima Publishing/St.Martin's Press, published annually). Gives in-depth advice and how-to tips, featuring extensive directory listings and profiles of literary agents as well as United States and Canadian book publishers and acquisitions editors. It's a great way to get acquainted with the likes, dislikes, and priorities of the people who make book publishing happen today; contains essays by literary agent Jeff Herman as well as a wide range of expert contributing writers.

Horowitz, Lois, *Knowing Where to Look: The Ultimate Guide to Research* (Cincinnati: Writer's Digest Books, 1984). An invaluable tool for anyone who has to dig up elusive facts and figures.

Huddle, David, *The Writing Habit: Essays* (Layton, UT: Gibbs Smith, 1992). A serious, useful book on the literary craft from a writer who wants to provide more than a how-to guide; practical, energetic, supportive advice and imaginative approach to learning tricks of the trade.

Kilpatrick, James J., *The Writer's Art* (Kansas City, MO: Andrews, McMeel & Parker, 1984). An opinionated discussion of proper usage, style, and just plain good writing from one of the news business's most popular curmudgeons.

Klauser, Henriette Anne, *Writing on Both Sides of the Brain: Breakthrough Techniques for People Who Write* (New York: Harper & Row, 1986). Tells you how to refrain from editing while you write; then how to edit, mercilessly and creatively, what you've just written.

Kremer, John, *Book Publishing Resource Guide* (Fairfield, IA: Ad-Lib Publications, 1990). Provides comprehensive listings for book-marketing contacts and resources—contains a vast bibliography and references to other resource guides. Look for newest periodically updated edition.

Kremer, John, *1001 Ways to Market Your Books—For Authors and Publishers* (Fairfield, IA: Ad-Lib Publications, 1986). Sensible, innovative, and inspiring advice on, first, producing the most marketable book possible, and then on marketing it as effectively as possible.

Literary Market Place (New York: R.R. Bowker, published annually). This is the huge annual directory of publishing houses and their personnel, as well as writing, editing, and publishing services nationwide.

Mann, Thomas, *A Guide to Library Research Methods* (New York: Oxford University Press, 1987). A practical guide to the most helpful, time-saving, and cost-effective information sources.

McCormack, Thomas, *The Fiction Editor* (New York: St. Martin's Press, 1988). How to fine-tune fiction; every bit as helpful for writers as it is for editors.

Miller, Casey, and Kate Swift, *The Handbook of Nonsexist Writing* (New York: Harper & Row, 1988). An excellent set of guidelines for eliminating sexist terms and constructions from all writing.

Namanworth, Phillip, and Gene Busnar, *Working for Yourself* (New York: McGraw-Hill, 1986). Everything you need to know about both the business and personal sides of freelancing and being self-employed. Great tips applicable to orchestrating a writer's business life.

Parinello, Al, *On the Air: How to Get on Radio and TV Talk Shows and What to Do When You Get There* (Hawthorne, NJ: Career Press). An exciting guide to the electronic media and its use for promotional purposes; ties in marketing aspects of such fields as seminars, social activism, and professional advancement—and is especially appropriate for authors with the entrepreneurial spirit.

Polking, Kirk, and Leonard S. Meranus, editors, *Law and the Writer* (Third Edition) (Cincinnati: Writer's Digest Books, 1985). A collection of pieces on legal issues that concern writers and their works.

Powell, Walter W., *Getting Into Print: The Decision-Making Process in Scholarly Publishing* (Chicago: University of Chicago Press, 1985). An eye-opening, behind-the-scenes look at the operations of two scholarly presses.

Poynter, Dan, and Mindy Bingham, *Is There a Book Inside You? How to Successfully Author a Book Alone or Through a Collaborator* (Santa Barbara, CA: Para Publishing, 1985). A thought-provoking series of exercises to help you assess your publishing potential.

Preston, Elizabeth, Ingrid Monke, and Elizabeth Bickford, *Preparing Your Manuscript* (Boston: The Writer, 1992). A contemporary guide to manuscript preparation that provides step-by-step advice for professional presentation of work for submission to editors, publishers, agents, television producers. Covers punctuation, spelling, indexing, along with examples of proper formats for poetry, prose, plays; also offers essential information on copyright, marketing, and mailing manuscripts.

Provost, Gary, *The Freelance Writer's Handbook* (New York: NAL/Mentor, 1982). Invaluable advice, mainly for writers of short pieces.

Rivers, William L., *Finding Facts: Interviewing, Observing, Using Reference Sources* (Englewood Cliffs, NJ: Prentice-Hall, 1975). A careful inquiry into the research process and the difficulties of achieving objectivity.

Roberts, Ellen E.M., *The Children's Picture Book: How to Write It, How to Sell It* (Cincinnati: Writer's Digest Books, 1981). A savvy and enthusiastic step-by-step guide by an established children's book editor.

Ross, Marilyn, and Tom Ross, *Marketing Your Books: A Collection of Profit-Making Ideas for Authors and Publishers* (Buena Vista, CO: Communication Creativity, 1990). Suggests fine-tuned, cost-effective, innovative promotional plans. Authors should note that the marketing strategy begins at the concept stage—before the book itself is written.

Ross, Tom, and Marilyn Ross, *The Complete Guide to Self-Publishing* (Buena Vista, CO: Communication Creativity, 1990). Up-to-date, step-by-step information and procedures on setting up your publishing business. Shows you how to take your book from the idea stage through production and into the hands of consumers. Not just for entrepreneurs who self-publish—contains valuable tips for commercially published writers to maximize the success of their titles.

Rubens, Philip, editor, *Science and Technical Writing: A Manual of Style* (New York: Henry Holt, 1992). A comprehensive one-stop style guide for writers and editors in scientific and technical fields (including students). Addresses fundamental issues of style and usage, discusses specialized terminology versus technobabble, and provides guidelines for communicating effectively to one's audience.

Seidman, Michael, *From Printout to Published* (New York: Carroll & Graf, 1992). Engaging and unvarnished consideration of the writer-publisher relationship from first draft through finished book. Details nuances of manuscript submissions, working with agents, contract negotiation, advances, editing, cover design, book marketing, promotion—and more.

Strunk, William, Jr., and E.B. White, *The Elements of Style* (Third Edition) (New York: Macmillan, 1979). This highly respected, widely read, and well-loved classic is seen by some contemporary writers as sheer stuffed-shirt punditry. It is, however, a slim volume and doesn't take up much space or time to read—and modern writers may well find themselves following the Strunk-and-White principles in spite of themselves.

Todd, Alden, *Finding Facts Fast* (Berkeley: Ten Speed Press, 1979). Detailed basic, intermediate, and advanced research techniques; hundreds of ideas for those stuck in a research dead-end.

Volunteer Lawyers for the Arts, *Pressing Business: An Organizational Manual for Independent Publishers* (New York: VLA, 1984). Delineates legal and business concepts applicable to smaller literary and not-for-profit publishing enterprises—addresses issues writers should be aware of, since for practical (including tax) purposes, they're in the same industry.

Sylvia K. Burack, editor, *The Writer's Handbook* (Boston: The Writer, published annually). One of the most respected, clear-eyed, high-quality publications in the writing-for-publication field; a pioneering work, now with a long tradition of success.

Writer's Market (Cincinnati: Writer's Digest Books, published annually). A directory of thousands of markets and outlets; best known for its listing of the hundreds of consumer and trade periodicals. Also includes

book publishers, book packagers, greeting-card publishers, syndi-
cates—and more.

Zinsser, William, *On Writing Well* (New York: Harper & Row, 1985). Shows
you how to simplify nonfiction writing and deliver fresh, vigorous
prose. An excellent book to keep on hand.

ABOUT THE AUTHORS

Jeff Herman is the president of the Jeff Herman Literary Agency, Inc., which he founded in 1985 at the age of 26. Herman is also author of the annually published book *The Insider's Guide to Book Editors, Publishers, and Literary Agents* (Prima Publishing). He frequently lectures throughout the country about how to get published.

Deborah Adams is an agent with the Jeff Herman Literary Agency, Inc., where she serves as resident book proposal doctor. In addition to an active career as an author, ghostwriter, and lawyer/mediator, Adams lectures on such topics as book proposal writing, spirituality, and the ins and outs of the writing life.

For information about lectures, other books, audios, and software products for writers by Herman and Adams, please call 1-212-941-0540. Or write: The Jeff Herman Literary Agency, Inc., 500 Greenwich Street, Suite 501C, New York, NY 10013.